Looking Back

True-Lee Short Stories

LEE SIMONICH

ISBN 978-1-64114-000-3 (paperback)
ISBN 978-1-64114-001-0 (digital)

Christian Faith Publishing, Inc.
832 Park Avenue
Meadville, PA 16335
www.christianfaithpublishing.com

Printed in the United States of America

For everyone who touched my life. To my sister Jeanne Black, Pearl friends Vicky Songer and Julie Walsh. Because of your nudges and words of encouragement…

In loving memory of Scott Biermann.

To Kerry Batchelder, on her kindness and devotion of copyediting with redlining. Thank goodness my favorite color is red. Kerry introduced the phrase, "one small bite at a time" to help me through the journey. I will always remember the words, "You're too quiet. I knew you were up to something."

Contents

INTRODUCTION

We have all been in broken places in life; emotionally, mentally and spiritually. We all have a past that follows us like a shadow. Lee found out a *Band-Aid* did not make the hurts in life feel better.

Embark on a journey with Lee as she peels back layers of her life, unleashing raw emotions in real-life moments.

After six years of seeds being planted, God finally let me know I was brave enough to write this book. It was then I asked myself, "How much do I tell? How deep do I go?"

Everyone has a story to tell. I did not ask for these chapters but they became my life story. The broken seasons are the reason I bow down and surrender my all to Jesus.

In letting go, God's mercy and grace changed her life to a keepsake. Treasures can be found in going through the simplicity and trials of life.

1

Why this Book

I never had a dream or passion to become an author until one day God placed in my heart a desire to paint a picture of being human through storytelling. It can only be explained, God is in control. There is purpose and a plan to let you see him at work through every situation and circumstance. Writing is generally a solitary art. I was privileged to have my friend Jesus cowrite on this collection of life stories through my eyes.

My family endured an unexpected loss after the sudden death of our father from an accident in 2008. My sister living two thousand miles away was my encourager on the journey to settle a loved one's estate. Jeanne wanted to send a journal book. She suggested that writing down personal feelings may help through this intense time of mourning and remembrance. I requested she not send the journal book; I had no time to journal while running a small business and all the other busyness that absorbs the hours in a day.

When the journal book arrived in the mail I could not believe she sent it against my request. The book was placed on a shelf in a closet and out of sight. Eight months later I retrieved the book and began writing down special memories shared with my dad.

While having lunch with a friend in 2011, I shared some of the highlights on a community project I was currently working on. Vicky expressed, "you should write a book as your life events are amazing." I could see a pattern developing over the span of event occurrences and the nudge to write by two people.

In 2014, during an afternoon coffee shop visit with a young woman it was again quite remarkable how we landed on book writing as the topic of discussion. Julie was showing me her Facebook page and there was a message about a relative's recently published words. Hearing of this success was another spark that ignited a fire in me. I began transpiring thoughts and reflections into the artistry of storytelling.

Breakthroughs in life come in God's timing and require patience and listening for His will in our life. Could the Holy Trinity be the significant sign for the number three between years and in bringing three individual's encouragement for the birth of this book: 2008 (3) 2011 (3) 2014 (3) 2017 (3) 2020.

During this journey I grew to hope, believe, trust and step out in faith on the promises of God. Nothing feels better than knowing I fully obeyed God's calling to be a storyteller. If the words written within the pages of this book inspire, encourage or impact even one life, I say "Hallelujah!"

2

Naomi

It has been ages since the days of Arlington Heights, Illinois. This one particular hometown memory of human kindness was the beginning link to my love walk.

At the age of twenty I went to the hospital emergency room for a post-tonsillectomy complication. The ER doctor completed the sutures to stop the bleeding and advised me to go home, rest and have someone spend the day with me. I was living with my sister Jackie at the time and did not expect her to miss a day of work to stay home with me. She had her own life responsibilities that included a mortgage payment each month.

Naomi a friend's mother was the answer to my caring needs for the day. She barely knew me yet offered to help when her son presented my predicament. I was still a bit shaken from the ER procedure upon my arrival at the home of my friend. The door opened and I was welcomed; however, I felt somewhat awkward being there. No matter how uncomfortable the situation seemed to be, Naomi's presence meant I would not be alone. In my mind, I calculated this kindness as being given because of the love of a mother for her son. My feelings of battling insecurity and uncertainty made me question why someone who is almost a stranger would be so kind.

My place to recuperate and rest for the day would be in the basement part of the house. Naomi's basement was completely finished and decorated bringing warmth to this large open area of space. Naomi walked downstairs to the basement throughout the day, checking in on me like a mother would do for her own children. There was no conversation between us, as the doctor's orders were absolutely no talking and plenty of rest for the day. This day opened my eyes to compassion. Naomi's random act of kindness always stayed with me and touched my heart.

I thought this was the end of the story until one day while listening to Christian radio on the drive into work, I heard the radio host talking about items that should be on a bucket list. She said, "Reach out to someone who made a difference in your life and tell them." This is much like a reverse bucket list from the traditional bucket list of one's own desires and wishes. I felt the words coming through the radio were being spoken directly to me.

God the Father does work in mysterious ways and allowed me not to fall into the spirit of fear, but to reach out and find Naomi after decades of silence. Courage is a virtue and sometimes it is okay to ignore logic and follow your heart. God has taken me full circle with Naomi who is now the age of ninety-four. I have so much appreciation for Naomi's son and his willingness and graciousness to be the messenger of this story to his mother. Tom told me she was thrilled that I remembered her! No matter where you are today or what you have been through, it is never too late to tell someone they have made a difference in your life and to say "thank you."

I have often asked myself why I did not have a tonsillectomy as a child. Answer is: It was not in God's timing. People's paths sometimes cross for a reason and I now see this circumstance as a blessing from God. Spending the day with Naomi did not happen by coincidence. It was in God's plan for my life. Ah, now I reckon, a seed was planted for kindness way back then and became a part of the story of my life. The Word of God nourished this seed for the harvest.

Naomi's spirit reinforced in me, you really never know how a smile, kind word or a simple random act of kindness may make a bigger difference than one could ever know. Naomi's moment of caring left a positive impact far beyond anything I could have imagined. I am building a legacy of kindness that I will leave behind and I think of Naomi when inspired to do something kind.

~Remember to be a Blessing to Someone~

Lee,

I am so flattered and thrilled to hear from you after so many years.

I appreciate and thank you for the very kind words you wrote about me. It is an honor at ninety-four years of age to be remembered for making a difference in your life and mine.

Warmest regards,

Omi

Naomi

3

Hospital Blessing

*A*close family member was in and out of the
hospital for several months. The search to
find a surgeon willing to do the surgery was
the first challenge to be conquered. There is always a
risk factor associated with surgery and this was being
considered high risk. This would be Scott's second
heart bypass surgery. Scott had become a dialysis
patient along with becoming diabetic since his last
surgery ten years ago.

We often find ourselves asking the question, "What can we do to possibly assist our family or others who are desperately in need of help?"
Remembering the words, the Lord Jesus himself said,
"It is more blessed to give than to receive" (NIV). In
my heart I carried a desire to know how I was being
called to help. I made an offer to my sister Jackie to

stay the night at the hospital prior to Scott's surgery. She was in agreement with my suggestion to help out in this way. She would discuss this option with Scott and would circle back with me on his response.

It was Saturday afternoon and I was at the hospital visiting Scott. The telephone at the bedside rang, it was my sister. I heard Scott say, "Your sister will be staying with me." Scott said good-bye to his wife, then expressed his gratitude and appreciation for the offer to stay Sunday night at the hospital. My hope with staying would give everyone comfort and some much needed sleep, prior to an eight-and-a-half hour surgery to endure the following day.

A nurse stepped into Scott's room with questions to ask in regard to the scheduled surgery on Monday. One particular question and the answer I heard crushed my spirit in an instant. The nurse asked if there was any religious belief that would not allow him to receive a blood transfusion. Scott responded with, "Religion is way low on the priority list." I sat in silence and became suddenly saddened with what I just heard.

Prior to this day I had shared with my younger sister Pauline who is a Christian, my willingness to be obedient to the Holy Spirit. I wanted to share the Word of God and salvation with Scott before the surgery. After hearing Scott's response to the nurse, I sat quietly in the hospital room. I would pray to be led with the right timing to share God's gift with Scott. A plan was made and I would be returning to the hospital on Sunday night around 10:00 p.m.

When I arrived at Scott's room the other family members were saying their good nights. They would be back in the early morning prior to the 7:00 a.m. scheduled surgery time. It was just the two of us sitting together as a nurse entered the room. The nurse was going over the hospital surgical sterilization cleansing instructions. This process would take place in three stages, which would begin at 4:00 a.m.

I was prayerfully asking the Holy Spirit for the right moment to speak with Scott about receiving Christ. The wall clock showed 11:00 p.m. I wondered if Scott would be sleeping soon. Thoughts were tossing in my head, *What if he slept up to the 4:00 a.m. start time to prep for surgery?*

To my relief, Scott told me he was not tired. He began sharing stories with me I had never heard over the years. The words being spoken were of life moments he chose to share with me at this time. While listening, I prayed for the right time to share God's gift of eternal life with him. A few minutes after the strike of midnight I just knew in my gut and sensed the Holy Spirit's presence leading me to be bold and step out.

I began by saying, "In our journey through life, none of us know when our time on earth will run out. I do know because of accepting Christ as my Savior, eternal life in heaven awaits me." I shared with Scott, accepting Christ is the simplest and most powerful invitation we can receive. I told Scott I loved him and asked if he would pray with me to receive Christ into his heart. Without hesitation, his reply was yes.

I closed my eyes and said, "Repeat this prayer after me," as I held his hand. "Lord Jesus, come into my life. Jesus, I believe in you. I want you in my life. Forgive my sins. Cleanse me from everything that is not right and make me a brand-new creature. Wash me clean. I believe you died for me and I believe you rose from the dead. Come and live in my heart. I give myself to you. I receive you Jesus and I thank you, I am now saved."

Scott showed a peaceful calmness on his face and was fast asleep within minutes after praying together. I gave praise and said "thank you" to God. I had just settled into opening a book to read when Scott's brother Tom entered the room. This brother was at the hospital earlier that night and said his good night with the other family members. Tom told me he could not sleep and decided to come back to the hospital. He asked how long his brother had been sleeping, I told him he had just fallen asleep. I did not share with him what happened, I did not know if he was a believer.

It was now 3:00 a.m. and I had not yet closed my eyes. I stepped out in the hallway and took notice of a woman in the adjacent room. She was sitting up in her chair and watching TV. I moved to the entry of her hospital room door and said, "Hello." Before long, I was standing in her room and we were talking. This woman had a pink heart-shaped pillow laid across her chest. This was her first day in this room after spending three days in the cardiac intensive care unit.

Through conversation we discovered her surgeon was to be Scott's in just a few hours. I asked if she had family visiting her in the hospital and she replied, "Yes, my husband and friends from my church." I asked the name of the church, it sounded as though it may be of Christian faith. I asked if she was a Christian and her reply was yes. Without any hesitation I replied I was a Christian. The next thing to happen was a gift for me. She asked if Scott was saved.

As the tears began to roll down my face, I replied with, "Yes, he received Christ into his heart just a few hours ago." With one hand holding the heart-shaped pillow against her chest, she raised her other hand up and gave praise and glory to our Savior. I could see by her facial expression it took all her physical strength. I was in awe to witness the determination and gracious attitude of this woman who showed her love for Jesus. It penetrated my heart to see how this woman was bold enough in God to ask a stranger if a family member had Christ in their life.

Pauline was the first of the family members to arrive at the hospital room prior to surgery. It was early and the sun was just beginning to come up, the time on the clock was showing 5:30 a.m. We were both glad to see Scott had fallen back to sleep after the completion of the last sterilization shower. We were standing in the corridor outside Scott's room when my sister started out with small talk. She quickly leapt into asking if I had the opportunity to talk with Scott. I knew exactly what she was asking of me. My reply to her was, "Scott accepted Christ." We both embraced each other and began sobbing with tears of joy.

The remainder of the family began to arrive; it was soon time for Scott to be moved to the surgical floor. The family began to walk with the surgical nurse down the hallway. I stopped at the room next door and took a peek inside. It was peaceful to see the woman was resting and sound asleep in her bed. I said a good-bye to her under my breath, knowing an angel must have placed her there just for me.

I stayed with my family as we all were allowed in the presurgical waiting room with Scott. It was heartwarming to hear Scott talk to his two sons and without a quiver in his voice express his expectations of them to help their mother if he should not survive the surgery. The surgeon said to his team, "Let's go do this," and Scott vanished from our sight.

With no sleep, I headed home to catch a few hours of rest before joining back up with those who would be waiting at the hospital. I asked Pauline to share with Jackie the wonderful news of Scott being a believer. I hoped this would give her peace. Scott's physical life was dependent upon the vital necessity of a heartbeat, while his eternal life was now secure with God in the Promise Land.

4

Busy

We live in a fast-paced world…

Too often we miss out on the miracles of the moment because we are too busy to take notice when they are present. I have no one to blame but myself for missing out on the things that God is doing and the things God wants me to do.

Slow down and relax is a simple message but difficult to learn and practice. When we are asked what we have been doing, we say, "Busy." The word "busy" describes our daily routines, with overpacked schedules and not enough hours in the day.

Here is my spin, which validates we have become just too busy. The traditional wedding invitation has become preempted with a "Tying the Knot-Save the

Date" portrait announcement card. This is sent out several months in advance of the wedding day. Was someone clever with this wedding marketing strategy, or is it the plain simple truth we live a busy life?

Two friends and I worked on a community project together in which we met every month for a meeting. We volunteered our time and met after working hours. After the successful completion of the project, we noted how we had made the time to schedule for business, but were not making the time for our friendship. This is how *girls' night out* came to be and ruled out busy. This social event is shared between three friends to have dinner out once a month. Joanne, Cindy and I enjoyed this special time together.

Another way I controlled busyness was scheduling a day and designated time to call a friend living out of state. We called it our tea time together across the miles. We talked for an hour or longer with no life distractions. During this time, I enjoyed my cup of tea while Kerry enjoyed her coffee.

With the Christmas season here and the baking of my favorite cookie recipe, I was in need of butter. The grocery store that is my routine place to shop offered a coupon featuring butter on sale. Upon my arrival at the store I found it was sold out. Near my place of work is the same store chain; I decided to stop there in hopes of purchasing the butter at the sale coupon price.

Entering this unfamiliar store, I saw the refrigerated cases and started walking in that direction. I was looking at the items but did not see any butter. There was an elderly man with a small grocery cart nearby. I approached him with a smile on my face, saying I was not familiar with this store. I asked if he knew where the butter could be found. The man was smiling as he spoke to me. He asked me to follow him and he would show me where to find it. He began pushing his grocery cart and a feeling of impatience overcame me, his steps were slow and this could take forever. I was in a hurry to get back to work at the office. I took a deep breath, realizing I needed to enjoy the moment and shared in conversation with the old guy. Once the butter was in my hands, I said a farewell to him. When I made it back to work and was taking a morning break with the crew, I shared my experience at the grocery store. I thought I had made his day but actually he really made mine.

I am sure this has happened to others when the time and the days slip by because busyness takes priority. An e-mail was sent to a friend at the beginning of the year saying, "Let's try to target a date in

February for a visit." The friend's reply was received the same day with a message saying she would work on a possible date and circle back with me. Some friends have been cut loose during my life's journey, but this friend was a keeper. After months had passed and never hearing back, I was fighting a battle with the enemy. My hesitation was if I should write another e-mail; it came with risk and vulnerability of rejection. I sent the e-mail with the words, "Please do not forget me. It has been forever and I hope to see you again." The friend's reply was, "I could never forget you." We met for lunch and had a grand time together with plenty of laughter. I did receive affirmation we would be forever friends.

On a late Thursday afternoon, I was diligently working to complete all of my tasks at hand prior to the start of the weekend. The work shift was working four ten-hour days. I could see a truck out of my office window that had parked. Out of the vehicle came a friend with an older woman. My first thought was oh no, I did not have time for an unexpected drop-in visit. I had my own agenda, which was to finish my work. Steve had recently moved his parents from North Carolina to make Arizona their new home for retirement. I assumed this woman must be his mother, whom I had never met over the years of being friends. Introductions were made, then Steve made his way to the shop area to visit the guys.

The woman began by telling me how great her son was for being involved in their relocation process. Before arriving they were at the senior center getting her registered for participation in activities. Through this she would be given the opportunity of meeting new friends. Her words to me that day were of their three sons, Steve had the biggest heart. She made sure to share with me she loved them all, but this particular son was dearly special and different than the other boys.

I found myself enjoying my time with her and did not think about the work waiting for me at my desk. The conversation flowed from both of us with ease as if we had already known each other for some time. To my surprise she asked if she could give me a hug. We embraced and she told me I was a wonderful person. She shared how her husband was utilizing his time in their golden years. I listened to her words, realizing I could have been looking in a mirror. I received a phone call later that evening from my friend. He shared how much his mother talked on the ride home about meeting me and how much she enjoyed our visit together.

I would have missed all of these moments if I had allowed busyness to control my life. I learned a valuable lesson in my later years. It is the little things people do for each other that ultimately mean the most. I now focus on who I can help today, who I can bless today, who I can encourage today and what I can give.

5

Homeless

A city park sat directly across the street from my work place. Being a small business owner, I was fortunate to be able to bring my four-legged best friend Reba with me each day. It was a daily ritual for us to walk at the park twice a day. We walked these park grounds for ten years and never saw anyone that appeared to be homeless or sleeping in the park.

It was about a month prior to moving the business location to a new city. While on our daily walk, something different happened. We rounded a familiar corner and came upon a petite woman perhaps in her midthirties. She was sitting by the sidewalk with two bicycles. The bicycles were packed with stuff. One had a cart being pulled behind and the wheel appeared to be broken from the frame. I noticed she had a dog that was leashed and decided not to take Reba in that direction to avoid the possibility of any dog confrontation.

On our second walk of the day we went the same direction and the woman was still there. Although this time I did not see the dog. For some reason instead of walking by I asked if she needed some help. The woman replied in saying her husband had left to try and find parts to fix the broken wheel on the cart. I told her when her husband returned, he could come by my place of business to see if we may be able to assist him in the repair of the wheel. Heading back I did see her dog, she had moved him into the shade up around the bend.

Going out in the world, I am usually cautious and reluctant to approach a stranger and especially one that may be homeless. Because I had no fear overcome me, God touched my heart to do an act of kindness for this woman.

Walking with my dog I thought about how blessed I am to have a place to live and a car to drive. I could not imagine being homeless and having no family or friends to take me in. Maybe this couple had made decisions in life to cause people to give up on them. I made my way back to work and told the guys that Reba and I had met a homeless woman at the park. I let them know I had offered our services to fix a broken wheel. Several hours had passed and I assumed they did not need help as no one came by.

Late afternoon and the shop bay door was open, we had a visitor ride up on a bicycle holding a wheel. One of the guys shook hands with the man and began to assess the problem. The welder was turned on, a bearing was replaced and he had to fabricate and weld another part to make it work. The homeless person told us what a blessing this was, as they had been stranded. He rode off on his bicycle and was told good luck. The homeless man called back, saying, "I do not believe in luck, but I do believe in God." I shouted back to him, "Angels too!"

In the days that followed, on our morning walk I continued to see this couple and their dog sleeping on the ground in their sleeping bags. The dog was always quiet and never barked at Reba and I as we walked by. In the afternoon walk, I would see them up and about at a picnic table under the shade of the trees. We always had some conversation together after a cordial greeting. Some days their belongings were there and they were nowhere to be seen around the vicinity. Through our conversations, I learned she was an artist. Gwen would go to the local street market to sell her pencil drawings. Jason her spouse tinkered with electronic repairs which contributed to their survival on the street.

Bringing a large-sized dog biscuit for their dog became part of our daily walk routine. Being a dog lover myself, I took notice of two dog bowls with water and dry food set out every day for Roland. The dog appeared to be well taken care of. I realized the three of them were a pack, devoted to one another. One particular day our conversation led me to ask for permission to walk freely into the space they called home. I wanted to be welcomed by them and respect what privacy they could possibly have in a public park. There was never a day they refused to engage in a visit with me.

The weatherman was forecasting some cold temperatures dipping down to freezing at night. It was the will of God to show Christ's love through me that someone cared. During that day's walk I handed the woman an envelope with enough cash to cover expenses to stay out of the elements. The next few days while walking in the park with Reba there was no sign of them and their belongings were out of sight.

The weather turned and once again I saw them at the park. They graciously thanked me as the woman asked, "How come every time I talk with you I cry?"

Thank you comes in many forms: words, smiles, laughter and tears.

No one can go back and start a new beginning, but anyone can start a new ending. Happiness for me lies in caring for others and giving to them. Becoming a giver has brought me levels of a joy-filled life I never knew possible.

6

Collectibles

We live in a throwaway society and the rage is to go greener with recycling programs. It makes me think of being a kid when there were enthusiasts on collecting baseball cards, comic books and coins. Times certainly have changed with tattooing and piercing for body adornment of anything imaginable, also being considered a collectible form of art.

The hobby of coin collecting is a lot of fun for kids, adults and families with collecting the state and park series quarters. I had the opportunity to begin my collection as a young child. My first acquired coins were quarters found in a slot machine that became ours through a trade of dad's hunting shotgun. I filled four quarter-album coin collector folder books with old dated silver quarters found within the slot machine.

A girlie girl I was not and I did not play with dolls. The design of how the slot machine works intrigued me with its elaborate configuration of gears and levers. The central element is a metal shaft which supports the reels. This shaft is connected to a handle mechanism that gets things moving. A braking system brings the spinning reels to a stop and sensors communicate the position of the reels to the payout system. I learned how to bypass the coin detector that registers a coin after it has been inserted and unlock a brake so the handle can move. After pulling the handle there is a clunk and the three reels start spinning. Then the three reels stop abruptly, one at a time to build suspense for the player. If the first reel stops on the jackpot symbol you have to wait for the next reel to stop to see if it is a jackpot and finally the third. This old slot machine was played with more than any other toy or game when I was a kid.

The classic mechanical design of this slot machine has been replaced by new technology. The computer controlled electrical machines reels are spun by motors and the stoppers are generally activated by solenoids. The modern slot machines have flashing lights and sound displays to entertain the player.

My youngest sister and I shared
together when growing up as kids. I kep
collection in the closet of our bedroom a
year younger sibling hit the jackpot w]
covered it. We had a Ben Franklin store up the road
from where we lived. My sister began to visit there
quite frequently on her own. The store clerk was a
mature person and probably took notice of the silver
quarter coins she paid with for the candy purchases.
I guess you could say the store clerk was the second
person to hit the jackpot. Most of the silver quarters
were gone from the coin collector folder books when
the discovery was made by me. After many tears I was
no longer inspired to make coin collecting a lifetime
hobby and closed this chapter of my life.

The memory of the loss of these coins was
replaced when I was presented with a commemo-
rative 9/11 coin from the mayor of my hometown.
I received it in recognition of our partnership for a
project to better the community. Another blessing
came my way when my neighbor began to give me
collectible coins for Christmas and birthday gifts.
A family tradition of James's was to give his broth-
ers and sisters a silver coin at the annual memorial
celebration for his beloved father. I too became the
recipient of a silver coin and became a part of his

family through our years of friendship. Being given these coins holds a sentimental value and replaces the gambler coins.

I made a rule that if others wanted to give me a gift, all gifts were to be edible; with the exception of receiving a collectible coin. This collection of coins will be treasured throughout my lifetime and will one day become a collectible for someone else to cherish.

Muscle cars are another collectible classic and this era of American automobiles is enjoyed by all ages. My 68' Chevy Camaro has given me the opportunity to participate in classic car show events. It is fun sharing car stories with other collector enthusiasts and hearing the restoration journey of their historic vehicle.

There are many things that will disappear in time over the years. Collectibles last a lifetime to be shared from one generation to the next. There is a saying which suggests collecting memories not things, but sometimes things are what create the memories.

There is a belief that things happen in three's and I became the winner of the third jackpot. Through prayer I have been freed from any baggage of bitterness, unforgiveness, resentment and anger toward my sister and that was a blessing.

68 Chevy Camaro

7

Why, God?

I have to ask the question, "Why do bad things happen to good people?" We have all had real pain, disappointments and problems in life. Why God did two sisters suffer tragic losses on the same day but in different years?

I heard my sister's voice on the phone saying her nephew Danny had stepped in front of a train and taken his life. It was June 2, just days before his seventeenth birthday.

This is a topic that is rarely talked about because shame is attached to suicide. We would be shocked by the number of young teenagers contemplating suicide as an option. Because there is such shame attached for even thinking these thoughts, most teenagers will not come out and openly communicate this with you. Teenagers will not say, "This is what I am dealing with, can you help me?"

Many teenagers today are growing up in single-parent households, which leads me to ask myself if authority and father issues present a problem. In addition to this, I have to wonder if acceptance, peer pressure, rejection and sexual identity are issues facing teenagers. Bullying is definitely a prominent issue. Is it possible the social media devices we have today are drawing teenagers inwardly and further isolating themselves?

Is the physical cutting of themselves a key sign when a teenager is in trouble with hopelessness? Is this cutting a way for them to take that internal pain and externalize it and will it distract them from the real issues at hand? Has physical cutting become a form of coping that has gone way beyond that of fingernail biting?

Children and teenagers need a safe haven at home. The question is: How do we communicate hope to these teenagers? Maybe it is the simplicity of making time to listen to our children and not just talk at them.

These were my words spoken to my sister Jeanne: "When we do not have the answers to tragic times in life and do not understand why things happened, our faith is severely tested. We must believe and trust in God during this season of sorrow and great loss."

There was silence between us and words were not spoken. We both remembered how June 2 had marked the loss of another child in our family from meningococcal meningitis. This is a rare infectious disease more common in children younger than five years of age. We were both powerless to save a child and needed each other for this day when grief visited our hearts.

I heard it said, if you lose your spouse, you're a widow or widower. If you lose your parents, you are an orphan. What do we call someone who has to bury a child?

God has placed this upon my heart to share our loss as a way of possibly touching someone else's life. When a child dies, the suffering is endured with the unconditional love of God.

With 365 days in a year, how does one day in June become the marking of an end of two precious lives and the beginning of another life dedicated to honor and serve our country in the military?

June 2 will always be a day remembered for both losses and blessings. My nephew's military orders were to depart for navy base camp in Illinois the same day.

8

Friendship

My hope is I am never too busy with schedules and responsibilities for friendship. It is a priority for me to stay connected to my friends and let them know I care. I do not normally make New Year's resolutions but have decided to dedicate this year to my friendship with others. My goal is to sustain friendships, not letting them dwindle away in the busyness of life. A true friend makes time for others and I want to have face-to-face communication with the ones I love.

The apostle John wrote, "I have much to write to you, but I do not want to use paper and ink. Instead, I hope to visit you and talk with you face to face, so that our joy may be complete."

Not all friendships are the same. I have my circle of friends I refer to as treasured friends and those

I refer to as acquaintances. Of my forever friends, Anita is the one I have known the longest. We do not see each other often due to living in different states, but have shared in many special memories. One was a lifetime adventure to Australia to visit our families. This friend is someone who encourages, trusts and believes in me. She is a forever friend that God himself has chosen for me.

My idea of an acquaintance friend would be most like the type of friend found on the social network of Facebook. This form of media is a way to stay in touch with friends, but is not a meaningful contact relationship for me in my old-school mentality.

How grateful I am for the valuable gift of friendship I share with my circle of friends. I will never give up being the kind of friend that always has time in her life and space in her heart for my treasured friends.

My signature niche of inviting forever friends to join me as my guest for a concert event has become part of my legacy. Memorable moments last a lifetime, whereas many gifts are forgotten and fade from our memory as the years go by.

The era of my concert going days are over and I will always treasure the memories of these concerts with these special friends. The travel was sometimes by car and other times we enjoyed the ride on a train to the venue. One limo ride in particular comes to mind, as a group of six of us went to see Tina Turner taking her energy on tour for the first time in eight years. These are the artists I had the privilege of seeing with treasured friends: Wynonna, Kelly Clarkson, George Strait with Reba and Lee Ann Womack, Paul McCartney, Carrie Underwood, Lady Antebellum with special guest David Nail, The Judds, Taylor Swift, Hunter Hayes, Josh Groban, LeAnn Rimes, Cher with special guest Pat Benatar, Toby Mac and completing the list of artists is classical violinist Taylor Davis.

Some may say going to a concert is an extravagant gift. It is not about the gift, it is about these friends. They are of value and I care about them. I am always open to God using me to pour out blessings on others. My depth of friendship continues to grow with love and admiration with each treasured friend.

Thank you for being a true friend…

Concerts

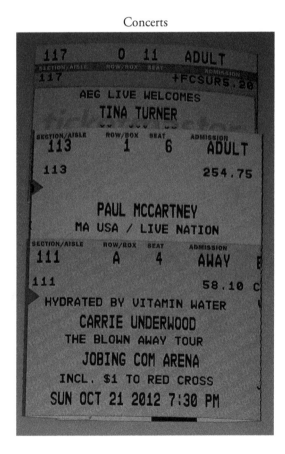

9

Military Letters

When my twenty-year-old nephew left for navy base camp in Illinois, I did not know he would be spending the next four years in Sasebo, Japan. Since I am old school I wanted to write letters the old-fashioned handwritten way, using the United States Postal Service to deliver the letters to him.

My business is driven by quarterly tax requirements, which I used as a reminder to write a letter each calendar quarter to my nephew. The letters consisted of a summary of the past three months activities, always closing with my signature trademark and a word of spiritual encouragement. I made sure to never ask questions of him in the letters. It would be impossible for him to carry out his service if everyone that loved him expected letters.

After serving his four-year term in the navy, I was invited to a surprise welcome home party for him. My nephew expressed his gratitude for all the letters he had received from me over that time period. He told me I was the most consistent in writing and said how much my letters had meant to him. I could not fight back the tears as I listened, knowing he was speaking genuinely from the heart.

It was hard to believe the handwritten letters stood up against social media, e-mail, Skype, texting and cell phones. There is still nothing like a hand-written letter with a postage stamp and the feeling you get from a real letter.

I later learned when Nick was packing his gear to come back home to the United States, he had saved every letter I had written especially for him. How long has it been since you last wrote a hand-written letter to someone you love?

This young man re-enlisted by personal request and will continue to serve our country. I believe he will achieve a high level of success in his life due to his great attitude; being humble, positive, responsible and thankful.

Because of him and all our military service men and women, I can exercise the liberty and privilege of prayer. May we never take our freedom for granted.

Special thanks to all who have served in the US Armed Forces...

Nick

10

Pearl Friend

The lovely and lustrous gem called a pearl is why I call a forever friend my pearl friend.

Each pearl is a different size, shape, luster and color just like my pearl friends.

How something so wondrous emerges from an oyster's way of protecting itself is one of nature's loveliest surprises. Some believed pearls to be the tears of the gods, others thought of them as dewdrops filled with moonlight that fell into the ocean and were swallowed by oysters.

Unlike gemstones or precious metals that must be mined from the earth, pearls are grown by live oysters far below the surface of the sea. Gemstones must be cut and polished to bring out their beauty, pearls need no such treatment to reveal their loveliness. Pearls have a shimmering luster and soft inner glow unlike any other gem on earth.

The birth of a pearl is truly a miraculous event. A pearl is a natural gem created by a living organism and a pearl friend is a natural beauty created by God.

To find perfectly matched high-quality pearls, a processor may sort through thousands of beautiful pearls. The harvesting of pearls is time consuming as in one's time to find and become a pearl friend.

When I let God go to work in my life to have the right friends I needed, I was blessed with my pearl friends. Hope you will find a pearl friend in your lifetime.

I have chosen my pearl friends signature piece to be cherry and white cultured pearl bracelets. The bracelets are made up of button, baroque, oval and ringed potato shapes, for our chic pearl friend look. If you see a woman wearing cherry and white pearls on her wrist, you might just ask if she is a pearl friend. Just imagine if this were to catch on as the next big trend in signifying other pearl friend relationships throughout the world.

A Pearl is a Timeless Gift

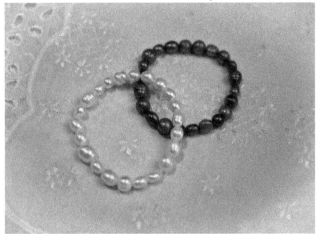

11

American Flag

I n August 2010, when visiting a friend's ranch, I saw the American flag being flown from the streetlight poles in the small rural town of Whitehall, Montana. The display of American flags spanned the main street of town. Upon my return home I wrote the editor of the *Montana Standard* newspaper. I learned that my words had been printed in "Our Reader's Speak" section. The newspaper editor named the article, "Montana flag displays are an Inspiration!" The article was printed word for word as it had been submitted to the editor. Here is a small portion of what was written: "Thank you Montana for this highlight of my visit and the reminder to be a proud American. Your state has given me the inspiration and vision to have my hometown start a flag program."

September marked the beginning of my journey in contacting the mayor of my hometown to share in this vision of patriotism. My morning call to the mayor's administrative assistant was welcomed with a kind voice. She asked what subject of discussion I was requesting with the mayor. I began by telling her how the state of Montana had inspired me with their exceptional display of the American flag. I told her I was committed with a mission to do the same in my hometown to honor our American heroes. City government was unfamiliar territory for me; with answered prayer a meeting was scheduled for January 31, 2011 in the mayor's office.

The meeting day arrived and both Mayor Lewis and his administrative assistant were friendly, which helped reduce the nervousness within me. I shared my vision to display American flags from our streetlight poles, thereby utilizing the streetlight for the illumination after dusk of our country's colors. During this meeting, Mayor Lewis expressed his love for the American flag. The discussion and possible direction regarding the addition of American flags to streetlight poles was placed as a Council Meeting Agenda Item on March 10, 2011.

Council Action: Discussion; possible action by motion

This process was certainly formal in comparison to the rural town in Montana, where local residents most likely installed the American flags as an afternoon project. My hometown of Gilbert, Arizona with a population of 229,972 residents was becoming a rapidly growing town. The challenge to follow the lead of this rural town in displaying the American flag along the downtown area was about to begin.

The town council meeting took place in March and I presented an overview of the flag program as I envisioned it. The funding for these flags would be provided through donations. Due to insurance liabilities and the town's ownership of the streetlight poles, the installation and maintenance of these flags would become the town's street department responsibility. A service fee would be determined by the town manager and paid for through donations, as to bring no additional cost to the town's financial budget.

At the conclusion of the meeting this agenda item was placed as an action item for the April 21, 2011 town council meeting. The "Contract for American Flags pilot program" as it was now labeled would be considered for approval. This would enable Mayor Lewis to execute the required documents. All council meetings are videotaped. When I later watched the online video of the meeting, I was pleased with my composure and presentation.

I attended the scheduled council meeting in April and watched as council members and mayor voted 7-0 for the American flag pilot program. I received an e-mail the following day from the mayor's administrative assistant saying, "Congratulations to you on the 7-0 vote. You have moved mountains and this is a tremendous accomplishment."

Seed money for the pilot program became available through local business donations, along with community participation in an Eagle Scout Fun Run Benefit. Upon completion of the pilot program the flag program was placed on the council agenda for October 6, 2011. Attending this meeting, to my surprise and others a group came forward with a dissenting opinion regarding the flag program.

Council Action: I was requested to schedule a meeting with this group to identify possible alternatives. After the meeting took place Vice Mayor Daniels had a telephone conversation with both groups, concluding there was no compromise or agreement to be met. The agenda item for approval of the flag program was rescheduled for the November 3, 2011 council meeting.

The topic of discussion during this council meeting was whether or not to place eighteen American flags along American Heroes Way, as a permanent site location. The recommendation was presented by vice mayor and I was in agreement. Vice Mayor Daniels gave her motion to put this agenda item to a vote. Each council member spoke of their own feelings of patriotic love for the flag. Each shared their personal and close family experiences in the military and why they were going to vote yes for this agenda item.

During the first week of December 2011, the flag program was implemented. These eighteen American flags will represent a visual reminder of our gratitude to our heroes. The flags fly 24/7 from the streetlight poles lining the mile stretch of road named American Heroes Way and the site of the 9/11 Memorial at town of Gilbert Town Hall. Our country's colors are illuminated from dusk until dawn according to proper flag etiquette.

Because of a vision that started in September 2010, these American flags fly to honor our heroes; both military and first responders in my hometown. The presence of these flags serves as a reminder for each heroes service and sacrifice.

This opportunity offered a life challenge in which I often found myself saying this simple prayer, "Walk with me Jesus on this journey." Throughout this experience, I have learned if you believe you can achieve and never give up. All things are possible with God.

My hometown came forward and requested ownership of the flag program in February 2013. An e-mail was received from the fire chief saying, "I am pleased to witness daily the effect of the flags on American Heroes Way. It was a pleasure to partner with you on this project and we will watch over these flags as the emblems they are." Another e-mail came from Mayor Lewis saying, "Your vision did become a reality and we are a better community because of you."

With my passion and determination, a young man's Eagle Scout project for the cause and two forever friends' help and support, we together made a difference in the community to honor our heroes. Operation Welcome Home, held at Gilbert Town Hall provides a heroes welcome and celebration for returning military and their families. The backdrop presence of these flags is one way our community says "thank you" for each heroes sacrifice.

12

Poison Pen Letter

Have you ever known someone who has received a poison pen letter? A poison pen letter is a letter or note containing unpleasant, abusive, or malicious statements, or accusations about the recipient. Poison pen letters are usually composed and sent to upset the receiver and are usually sent anonymously.

In my experience, the relationship I had with an individual went from them telling me I was a wonderful gift to them and their life was better because I was in it, to being the recipient of a poison pen letter.

Could a letter like this be associated with feelings of guilt, rejection, anger or fear? Or is the underline cause resentment, bitterness, unforgiveness or an addiction to alcohol and drugs? For some people their problems have become their lives and they would not know how to spend their time without them.

I invested time and energy over the years into helping a person, but they really did not want to change. I could not let her make me feel guilty because I knew I followed God, not only in trying to help but also in letting go. In order to establish a boundary of keep out, I had to allow no further communication between us.

She was known to have a pattern of behavior in the writing of poison pen letters to others. She was predictable and stayed true to an unkind demeanor. One day in the mailbox I found her poison pen letter addressed to me. I made the decision that day not to open the envelope and to protect myself from being hurt by this individual. Someone I knew asked to read the letter. I agreed, only if they would shred it when done reading. I certainly did not want to hear or know anything that had been written in the poison pen letter. I was told the right choice was made in not reading the letter.

There are two forms of mail that can scare me, one being a letter from the IRS and a registered mail receipt, that requires a signature for pickup at the local post office. One day after arriving home from a day of work I went to the mailbox. Inside was a green registered mail receipt. The return address belonged to the person who wrote the poison pen letter a few years ago.

The day I decided to drive to the post office to retrieve this registered mail, I saw two young boys standing at the street corner holding signs for a car wash. A strong feeling came over me like an epiphany of sudden and striking realization to donate money for this cause. My bank just happened to be directly across the street from where the boys were promoting the car wash. After visiting the bank, I pulled in the parking lot where the car wash was being held and parked my car. I then walked over to a man who was helping the boys and asked, "Why the car wash?"

The man was the father of one of the boys washing the cars. He said they were raising funds for the boy's football team who just won a divisional championship. The football team was invited to New Orleans during Super Bowl week for a youth football training camp. I handed him a one-hundred-dollar bill and walked away without a car wash. In my heart, I knew this was a random act of kindness and a way to pay it forward. In the midst of my current trial, God had given me this divine opportunity to bless others. God's best was with me that day and I smiled as I had just received victory in this area of my life.

I left the car wash and made my way to the post office. The clerk handed me an envelope and I signed for the registered mail. Sitting back in the car I slowly opened the envelope. The letter said my name had been removed from her Last Will and Testament.

Years passed by, another card arrived with the return address of this same person. The outside of the envelope was imprinted with dogs. Since I am a dog lover the envelope was inviting. I found the letter confusing, she stated the letter was not written by her, although I recognized her handwriting. I'm guessing this may have been her way to fulfill Step #8 in a twelve-step program. Step #8 - Make a list of all persons we have harmed and become willing to make amends to them all.

I did write back. However, I was reluctant to reply to her note card because she had requested I never contact her. I wrote, we all have to be responsible for ourselves and have to own our problems as well as our behavior without placing blame on others. With seeking professional help as you have indicated, it appears you have made the decision for the need to do some things for yourself in your life that only you can do. I concluded the note in saying, "This may bring you comfort in knowing the original letter you wrote was never read by me."

I have recovered from this emotional excursion because the healer lives in the inside of me.

13

Unbroken

I grew up in a time when mothers ruled the home and were stay-at-home moms. Fathers roles were to work and provide the income for the family household. Fathers at that time were not involved in the daily lives of their children. Oh yes, fathers were often the disciplinary enforcer and how often we heard those words, "wait until your father gets home and hears about this."

I felt safe as a child in my home and loved by both parents. What was missing in my childhood was my own feelings of worth and value. I did not grow up well-grounded and this resulted in having a poor self-image. Shyness and being quiet became my personality traits. I did not talk unless spoken to and few words were said back to anyone who engaged in a conversation with me.

My father was a tradesman and worked outside in the cold winter elements of the Midwest. Because of this our family vacations were taken in the winter months and spent in a place where the temperatures were warm and the days sunny. I recall a winter vacation in Florida when my sisters were all having fun in the swimming pool. I was sitting alone at a pool side table doing school work. The memory still sits vividly with me after so many years. There is a black-and-white photo tucked away in the pages of our family photo album which depicts me doing school work on this vacation. School work did not come easy for me and I compared myself to my other siblings, as it seemed effortless for them.

I saw myself as dumb, stupid and not good enough, which bruised me with a dark side to my childhood. As a child, I did not understand how the evil enemy tries to fill your mind with negative thoughts to break you down. I needed to hear encouragement but could only hear the message of failure from the enemy and my mother. This bondage became a part of my life through my high school years and beyond.

A shift in my way of thinking of who I am as a person has since changed. I have peace and joy that no one can ever steal away because Jesus lives in me. I celebrate my life focusing on the good in me and honoring myself. I see myself as unique and special, created different from everyone else, no longer an empty shell. I live courageously, taking risks. The brokenness is gone and the renewed me is here to stay. God did not allow negative labels placed on me to ruin his purpose and plan for my life. I am not bulletproof, I now have assurance of a new suit of armor that will stand up to whatever tomorrow may bring.

I have also been set free from the chains that bound me through forgiveness for my mother. Through everything I have learned the value and destruction of words. Once spoken there is no taking them back. Words can be sweet and encouraging or cut deeply like a sword, leaving lifelong twisted impressions. I will always be mindful of my choice of words spoken to others.

We can choose not to be defined by our past scars and I am not a victim because I have the victory. I am proof, God is good! I believe in miracles, I am one.

14

Gold Star

Operation Welcome Home events in my hometown provide a heroes welcome and celebration for returning military and their families.

To attend this event is one way of saying "thank you" to a service person. I was standing along the sidewalk outside of town hall along with many others waiting to welcome home a particular hero. A woman and I began talking. She had two young children with her for the event. I heard a German accent in her voice.

I introduced myself and she told me her name as well as the names of the children. She said they had recently moved here from Germany and this was to be their new home. The woman was impressed on how the town honored its military heroes and showed support for the families.

This gave me the opportunity to share my passion with her about honoring our military heroes and first responders. I told her about the eighteen American flags, which were being flown along the one-mile stretch of American Heroes Way. She shared with me her spouse had served in the military in Germany. She also told me that she had phone contact with the council member who founded Operation Welcome Home, but had not met yet. She was hoping to meet her at this event.

The hero and his family arrived and all were waving American flags and cheering. The crowd began making their way to the entrance doors of town hall. I told her we would most likely get separated in the crowd and said it was a pleasure meeting her and the children. As we crossed the threshold into the building, I could see the council member this woman had wanted to meet within a few steps.

Councilwoman Daniels and I locked glances and immediately exchanged hellos. We had met previously when I was given the opportunity to attend town hall meetings with the Honorable Mayor Lewis and council members to approve the contract for placement of the American flags.

I had the privilege of introducing Council Member Daniels to this woman as we made our way through the lobby. While walking side by side, Councilwoman Daniels asked in a soft whisper if this woman was a Gold Star. My response was, "I did not know." I had no awareness of the term Gold Star.

Making my way into town hall, I took a seat and looked at the crowd still coming into the chamber. I saw the woman and the children entering and waved for them to join me. The chamber was filled to capacity to honor this hero. While sitting someone handed us a blank note card to write a thank-you to this soldier. We both wrote our sentiments as these cards would be given to him in a book. I could not help but notice the woman was in tears as we listened to the words being spoken to the soldier and his family.

At the conclusion of the ceremony, Honorable Mayor Lewis took the podium and asked a certain woman to please stand. The woman I sat next to rose from her seat. Mayor Lewis then paid tribute to a fallen soldier who was the spouse of this woman. I felt honored to give her a warm embrace as others acknowledged her sacrifice and gave hugs to this Gold Star recipient.

Military Gold Star – the Gold Star represents a military family member having been killed in action.

15

Impetigo

For those who do not know about impetigo, it is a bacterial skin infection that mainly affects infants, children and is rare in adults. After returning home from a visit out of state, red sores appeared under my nose. The sores broke open, oozed fluid and developed a yellow-brown crust.

I had these symptoms one other time as an adult, which was treated by a doctor with a triple antibiotic ointment cream. It was the weekend, I had two choices, go to urgent care or talk to my neighbor who is a pediatrician. I did not in any way want to overstep our neighbor-friend relationship, or his professional boundaries. I received peace it would be all right to send him an e-mail. Within minutes of hitting the send button, my cell phone rang. It was Dr. Carroll saying he read the e-mail.

He said to meet him at the back fence of our yards. This is a common area where we have met many times to talk and to exchange Christmas gifts and other goodies. This would be my first doctor visit in which I did not sit in a waiting room or pay a co-pay. Dr. Carroll took one look at me and confirmed I was 100 percent correct with my diagnosis of impetigo.

He handed me a prescription, I handed him a frozen Key lime pie for his family. I expressed how much I greatly appreciated his act of kindness. The property directly behind my home was a vacant acre lot for many years, until this family of eight became a special part of my life.

Another of God's Blessings

16

Dad

There is no bond quite like the one with my dad. He made a decision in his life to never be anything like his father, who was a mean old man. We were raised with family values and went to church on Sundays.

Most men will say they want a son. My dad was given the gift of four children, all being girls. Our birth names all had a slice of boy in them. My name was spelled like a boy's name, not the pretty girl way of Leigh.

Everyone has childhood memories to cherish; mine were extraordinary ones with my dad. Some of the best times in life happen when being a kid and those life experiences are remembered as footprints in the sand of time. My sisters and I enjoyed placing sponge curlers in our dad's thick Italian hair. The four girls had long thick hair, but for some reason never braided or styled each other's hair.

On Fridays we went to the YMCA for our family night. A favorite was the buffet dinner where we had a large variety of foods and desserts to select for our consumption. We all participated in roller skating, swimming, gymnastics and movies for the family's entertainment. My dad's patience was that of a saint while teaching me how to roller skate and playing ping-pong.

Our dad really enjoyed the horses and we became a horse race loving family. When our friends were at the soccer fields playing team sports on Saturday, we were at the racetrack with our dad. Mom stayed home and had the day to herself, which was a much-deserved break from us kids. Horse racing was an outing for us girls and admission to a racetrack was often free. It could have been called a school day of learning quinella, trifecta and superfecta, as well as a day of gambling entertainment for dad. In the beginning I mainly picked the horses by their names and color. Then I learned the basics of how to bet on the ponies and reading the odds of it winning next to its name. If I was of age to bet I would have been called a straight wager, meaning you only bet on one horse to win, place, or show. Being children we had fun there and would pick up all the losing race tickets from the ground. We never considered all the dirt and germs being handled when we were kids just having fun.

Italian families like food and we had a favorite lunch place. They had the best hot Italian beef sandwich with grilled sliced green peppers. I will never forget the name of the place, it was called Booby's. I was young and not great at reading and spelling, thinking it may have been Bobby's. Later in life I found out it actually was Booby's.

All the kids in the neighborhood visited our home when needing a sip of water to quench a thirst when playing outside. We had a pure white porcelain drinking fountain installed outdoors because dad was a plumber. Those were the days when we drank water from the garden hose.

My love of dogs started from a little girl and carried through my adult years in life. Dad enjoyed duck hunting and raised beagles at our home for this sport. If a beagle was timid or afraid from the noise of a gun firing, they failed the test to become a hunting dog. Do you know what happens to a dog that cannot be used for hunting? In my dad's eyes they became the family pet, which resulted in a pampered life of living indoors and sleeping on my bed.

The other beagles had a working dog's life and stayed in kennel runs in the garage. We were not allowed to play with them. One unwanted beagle for hunting, became my best friend to cuddle and love. The beagle breed is known to love food and Cocoa saved me from eating foods I did not like. We were not allowed to leave the kitchen table until we cleaned our plate of all our food. Thank goodness Cocoa's calling and purpose in life was for the taste of food and especially her liking of green peas and broccoli.

Having my own business in my adult years gave my dad the opportunity to do frequent pop-ins at work. The work crew called him Grandpa Joe. They all enjoyed his visits as much as I did. We were supplied weekly with donuts and cakes dad brought in for enjoying at break time. He would spend time out in the shop area and view the equipment being fabricated for the nuclear power industry. We would then go into the office and have a hot cup of tea together and visit. This was a good time for him to give me any doctor bills to pay and bank statements to reconcile for him. Dad managed quite independently but did like having me handle all his finances. Once in a while we would go to the park located across the street and walk my dog Reba together. I will always remember my dad's teaching of old-school values, simplicity, integrity, kindness and financial responsibility.

I know what it is to have a great dad that listened during the times when I stood in a pool of tears. It was very easy to love my dad and to spend time with him. I miss him and somewhere over the rainbow I know he is there. As the days go by, I know my Heavenly Father will carry me through. I am blessed with the certainty of heaven and being with loved ones once again.

Dad

17

Football

This was to be a fun day as well as an experience shared with friends attending the Cardinals vs. Broncos football game at the University of Phoenix Stadium. A local restaurant was having their Second Annual Pub Crawl to the Cardinal's game. This event provided transportation through a privately hired bus to pick up the fans at each designated location. An e-mail was sent out prior to the Pub Crawl with the scheduled departure times at each restaurant. The Pub Crawl package included a ticket to the game and a lunch to be served at the last pickup location.

Those participating in the Pub Crawl were allowed to bring along a cooler of their own selected choice of alcoholic or nonalcoholic beverages to enjoy on the bus ride. I considered the hired bus a designated driver for those wishing to partake in alcoholic beverages. At our final pickup location I watched the clock as we ate lunch. Seeing the minutes slip by, I searched out the bus driver and asked when the bus was due to depart. It was past the one o'clock departure time. We finally boarded the bus and I knew we might be late for the start of the game. To make matters worse the driver did not arrive at the correct stadium entrance for designated bus parking. More time went by as the driver maneuvered the bus through traffic to its properly designated parking area.

I walked fast from the parking lot to the stadium entrance and entered the security checkpoint line. Our seats were in the nosebleed section and the game clock showed nine minutes and fifty-two seconds left in the first quarter. My heart sank, I realized I had missed the singing of our National Anthem, which would have been the highlight of my day.

Some friends in our group attending were not football fans but came along for the experience of the new stadium. They ventured off to tour the surroundings leaving myself and a friend, who loved football as much as I did to watch the game together.

A fan sitting in the seat in front of me was the owner of the restaurant that sponsored the Pub

Crawl. He turned around to ask how I was enjoying the game. I told him I was disappointed with the bus arriving late for the start of the game and missing the singing of our National Anthem. He wanted to engage in further conversation with me and I politely asked him to please turn around. This may have agitated him, as he did not turn around, but continued talking. He then offered to buy me an alcoholic beverage to make up for my disappointment.

I declined the drink offer and he became angry. He asked his buddies if they had money to give him in order to refund my Pub Crawl package. Handing me the cash he and his friends stood up and exited the row.

Our group soon returned and my friend told them about our incident while they were away. My concern was whether I would be allowed to board the bus for the ride home. Well, if refused, I now had his $100 to pay for a taxi ride. The Cardinals won the game with a score of Cardinals 43 and the Broncos 13. My friends and I reached the bus and climbed aboard sitting toward the front. The back of the bus was filled with fans that had enjoyed the game with the assistance of alcoholic beverages. They were loud and hollered up to us, "The front of the bus sucks!"

Something else happened the day of going to this football game. When a day turns bad or not as planned, there sometimes is a sunshine moment when least expected. When walking up to the security checkpoint, I noticed a familiar face. A young girl I had worked with and had lost touch with over time. We quickly exchanged phone numbers and hugged, making our way through the security checkpoint.

There was a reason for being at this football game and God's timing is perfect. There is no other way to explain our meeting each other when there were 63,400 football fans in attendance and many entrances into the arena. Through this encounter we have stayed connected and Julie has become like a daughter.

Julie

18

Like a Mother

Not everyone has a beautiful and exceptional lifetime relationship with a mother. For those unfortunate ones, there is the chance of finding like a mother.

Sometimes a mother's time spent here on earth is cut short. My mother lost her battle with cancer when I was in my twenties. There are four girls in our family and two of my sisters had a wonderful mother and daughter relationship. My relationship with my mother could have been described as a piece of glass on a rocky road. Our glass was not smudge-free and sometimes our glass did not stay whole but became cracked, broken, or shattered.

I did not love my mother like someone who should be able to love their mother. She was a good mother, the best she knew how to be. Always grateful and thankful to her for the gift of life.

Many families have disconnected family members for different reasons, but life goes on. Some families become a blended family after the death of a parent, or when a divorce happens between parents. There is also no guarantee a mother's love and bonding will occur when the two worlds merge into one.

For me, like a mother happened miles away from home in the country of Australia. Love stories do happen. My dad and this lovely woman wrote a beautiful love story together. I was fortunate to share life with them, both in the United States and down under in Australia. With the seasons being opposite of one another they shared the best of both worlds. They were able to spend six months a year in each other's country while staying connected with both families.

Tucked away I have a special memory of a beach kiss shared between the two of them. I recall the glow on both of their faces which brings me back in time to the innocence of a first kiss. I could only hope to have that kind of love call upon my heart one day.

Trish was like a mother to me because we simply did life together. I remember when we purposely woke up at 5:30 a.m. to share the sunrise together on the beach. The time we burnt the breakfast croissants in the oven because we were engrossed in talking politics. When we walked up to the lighthouse through bushy paths, we never thought about the chance of an encounter with a snake in our path.

I snagged a favorite sweater and the yarn was pulled out in a long string. Trish had that special way of fixing the sweater to make it look like new again. I remember a mom moment with a bowl of soup being made and served bedside when feeling sick with a cold during an Australian visit.

One afternoon outing resulted in a DUI Task Force Sobriety checkpoint stop. Trish followed the officer's instructions and took the breathalyzer blood-alcohol test. She was not an impaired driver. I asked the Australian police officer to test her a second time for a photo shot of a lifetime. The officer smiled, ah… now I reckon the police officer probably thought I was a crazy American. The officer and Trish complied with the request of a second breathalyzer blood-alcohol test.

Most of all, we have shared our hearts together on life's journey with a closeness and depth to our relationship. I can drop my guard and tell her my secrets with no fear to be judged or thought less of when everything is exposed. She believes the best of me and makes me feel real love in my life. We are connected for life and I love Trish for giving the gift of like a mother to me.

There was another special gift I received from Trish, a teddy bear. This stuffed bear expressed shared love between my dad and her. The thirty-year-old bear was passed down to me during my last home visit to Australia. Hopefully to continue the legacy with a love story of my own. A friend shared these words about my bear, keep him close and watch what happens. Good things!

Lee,

Like a mother brought a tear to my eye. I can add little to your prose, except to say I am honored to be your very own Like a Mother and in return say that you are my Like a Daughter, and there is so much more I could share with you if we were situated to spend more time together.

Love and hugs,

Trish

Trish and Lee

Bare Bear

19

Thirteen

The number 13 proved to be a lucky number, not merely a numerical superstition as many believe. I found this to be true when it came to finding an industrial condo asset purchase.

The leased building where my company was operating went up for sale. Questions arose when seeing the For Sale sign in front of the building. Would the new owner require all the building space for his sole purpose? Would there be an option to continue the lease? With a drop in the economy and no sign of a recovery in sight, it could take time for a prospective qualified buyer to come along.

The first three years with the current owner consisted of a signed lease agreement. The following six years was agreed upon with a gentleman's handshake. With a new owner it would most likely be a requirement to sign a lease agreement with the possibility of a monthly rent increase.

The company was generating a positive cash flow and a decision was made to take a bold step of faith. I decided to pursue a future plan for the business with a building expansion and relocation.

When reviewing the industrial condo listings sent over from the real estate agent, one newly constructed building caught my eye. It displayed curb appeal, covered parking and a fenced private yard. This industrial condo unit had two major strikes against it. Inadequate electrical power to run the equipment and the suite number being 113. Because of these drawbacks the listing was placed in a stack of undesirable properties to view.

After working a full day, it was then onto spending a few hours in the evenings with the realtor. Our search resulted in a limited number of buildings meeting the square footage and electrical requirements. None were new construction, except suite 113.

Taking a drive one day in the surrounding area of my home, I discovered an industrial complex with condos available for purchase. The available sizes of units were a few hundred square feet smaller than the desired need of the business operation facility. The pluses were a short distance from home, competitive sale price, fenced private yard and new construction. Additionally there was access to a semitruck loading dock. There were also no covered parking areas. In Arizona it is highly desirable to park your vehicle out of the direct sunlight.

I took a drive to the building at night to see how well the outside of the building and parking area were illuminated for security. There was a pickup truck parked by the garbage dumpster and a person was unloading trash. It is a common practice for nonowners to come to an industrial site and dispose of garbage during nonbusiness hours. When I confronted him he told me he was an owner in the complex.

Cordial conversation began to take place between us. It is a small world as the conversation led me to say this building was a short distance from where I lived. He proceeded to say he was a licensed contractor and had built a few custom homes in the surrounding area. We established he was the builder of my home. I applauded his workmanship and the quality.

The realtor was contacted and an offer was written up. A contract was submitted a few days later to the building owner's investment group. The owners did not accept the purchase offer nor did they counteroffer. I was becoming discouraged with the search for an industrial condo. With the summer months only six months away the time to move was now, before the heat rolled in.

The real estate agent suggested talking to Doug, the owner adjacent to suite 113, who was the electrical contractor for the industrial complex. A phone call was made and he confirmed there was power available in the main electrical box to run additional lines to suite 113 for the equipment requirements. Doug was friendly and offered to make sure the conduit lines for wiring were not blocked from construction debris. The inspection guaranteed 400 amps of power to the suite.

With two weeks lost on trying to purchase the other building, suite 113 was under a written contract with a potential buyer. The realtor suggested submitting a backup offer as the owner had not yet accepted the offer. My offer was submitted and within five days I was signing the purchase contract. Perhaps the other prospective buyer made a low ball offer because suite 113 had set vacant for many years after its completion.

There is more to the number 13, which is proven by history. In 1726, at the age of twenty,

Benjamin Franklin wrote a list of thirteen virtues to serve as a guideline for him to develop his character. Number thirteen states, humility. In the Bible, humility or humbleness is a quality of being courteously respectful of others. It is the opposite of aggressiveness, arrogance, boastfulness and vanity. Thirteen is the number of the original colonies and the American flag has thirteen stripes in honor of these first colonies. The Thirteenth Amendment to our United States Constitution abolished slavery. At funeral services of a military member, the American flag is folded thirteen times into a triangular shape before it is handed to the family in honor of their service and sacrifice. Each of the thirteen folds has a unique significance. A baker's dozen, thirteen, is that extra product thrown in for good measure. It was the baker's fear of incurring the penalty for selling bread that was underweight.

I made the choice to follow God's direction and not fall to a numerical superstition, suite 113 has been blessed.

20

Angels

There is a spiritual meaning to finding pennies. Pennies fallen from heaven are angels in spirit. When I arrived at work one day, I stepped out of my car and there at my feet was a clean and shiny penny. I had no reluctance in picking it up off the ground as it must have been meant for me. In the last ten years of parking in the same parking space, this was the first time I had found a penny.

I believed an angel had been sent to provide support, thereby enabling me to stand strong in the midst of a storm in life. The winds of adversity began to blow. The odds were stacked against my brother-in-law Scott to survive an eight-hour heart bypass surgery. With him being diabetic, a dialysis patient and his overall poor health condition, it was risky. He took up residence in the cardiac intensive care unit and spent four weeks in a deep state of unconsciousness after the surgery.

Scott was then transported to a long-term care and rehabilitation facility. A tracheal tube was put in place and hooked up to a ventilator as his condition required a machine to breathe. This has been known to cause an emotional toll on patients with serious illness, such as his. Not to mention the inability to communicate.

Sunday became my routine day to visit. MD Anderson was my visiting partner on most Sundays. The first hurdle to conquer was how we would communicate with Scott. Walking into his room I was guaranteed to be greeted with his smile. His illness robbed him of the ability to hold a pen and write. A little board containing the letters of the alphabet was our first means of trying to communicate with him. The process was slow and tiring for Scott as he would point to each letter in a word. At times it was as frustrating for him as it was for me. Under the circumstances his positive attitude was remarkable to witness. God gave me favor all along and the grace to go through it.

Because the patient's communication skills were limited, it was vital for family members to become Scott's advocate. Upon one Sunday arrival we noticed his bed air mattress was completely deflated. This had to be uncomfortable for him. Through our "point to letter" way of communication, we soon learned the bed had not held air for the past two days. It was determined the auto fill on the air mattress was not working and a new bed was brought in. The transfer and exchange of the bed was no easy task for the staff. There were two patients per room and it was difficult to maneuver a bed in and out of the small area. With frustration my thoughts carried me to wonder if it was an oversight on the part of the care center staff or neglect for Scott's care and comfort.

In the weeks to follow a special valve was attached to the tracheal tube, permitting speech. The air he breathed no longer passed through his voice box. His voice was like a whisper and I became good at reading his lips. The respiratory therapist allowed only short intervals of time for the valve to be in place. Scott was too physically weakened from his illness to withstand longer periods of time.

On Father's Day, MD Anderson brought Scott a gift of a stuffed dog. This was to remind Scott of Anne, his four-legged companion who was waiting for him at home. Each time we visited we noticed the stuffed dog was always next to his side on the bed.

I recall the Anne visits our family was blessed to have given Scott. There were strict rules to adhere by for Anne to be allowed to visit the hospital and long-term care centers. It was a group family effort to meet all of the requirements for Anne to visit. Anne had to be a well-mannered dog. They needed documents showing current vaccinations and she had to be given a bath a day prior to the visit. She was also required to be on a leash at all times during the visit. The nursing staff had heard about Anne from Scott and had seen her photo in his room.

She was greeted by name as she walked down the corridor to her daddy's room. Her visits were not only an out-of-the-park hit for Scott, but for all of the other patients who had the chance to see her. Anne was a rescue dog and Scott had given Anne a second chance at life.

Another memorable visit was the day we arranged for the staff to prepare Scott for an outdoor visit to the care center's patio. The instructions were to call two days in advance for this type of request to take place. MD Anderson made the call and was told by a staff member he would be ready upon our arrival on Sunday.

When we arrived and entered Scott's room, he was still in his bed. There was frustration on our part as they did not do what they had promised. Out to the nurse's station I headed and stayed calm while expressing my disappointment. Not much time had passed before two nurses entered his room with a hoist to lift him from his bed into a reclining wheelchair.

Scott enjoyed having lunch outdoors with us on this sunny, mild, beautiful day. We had the entire patio to ourselves to enjoy with him. While sitting on the patio, the lawn sprinklers turned on to water the surrounding grass and flowers. Scott heard the sound of birds and felt the sunshine on his body. This was his first time outside in months with the exception of medical transport from hospitals and care center facilities. There was no time limit on how long he could stay outdoors. The staff offered to replace the portable oxygen bottle if needed.

Our visits ended with asking Scott if it was okay for us to pray with him. He always said yes and the three of us held hands as we prayed together. His room had a window, through which he could look outside. We asked him to watch for us walking down the sidewalk when we left. One day we walked right up to the window of his room. Putting our faces to the glass, we smiled as we waved our good-byes.

One Sunday visit we were held up from leaving at our normal departure time. My one-acre property gave my dog Reba plenty of area to walk and sniff. On this particular day, she decided to take her time in finding just the right spot to leave a deposit.

There is a requirement to sign in at the front desk of the care center during visiting hours. The young girl attending the desk informed us the patient we were there to visit had just been taken a few minutes ago to the emergency room. The two of us left the care center and drove across the street to the hospital.

When we entered Scott's room a nurse was entering information on a computer. MD Anderson and I both moved to one side of the bed to comfort Scott. The nurse asked what our relationship was to the patient and asked about his medical history.

In my opinion Scott's condition was anxious, distraught and disoriented. He had no real recognition of us being present in the room with him. We both held his hands hoping our warmth and touch would erase the loneliness from his face. He was lying flat on his back and raising his arms up, moving them in a flaring motion. We each held one of his arms and lowered them to his side. His arms seemed unusually strong for someone who had lost his muscle mass because of his illness. He continued to raise his arms up. I spoke to him, saying, "It is Sunday, a day of rest.

You do not have to do any physical therapy exercises today." I do not know if he heard me or understood a word of what I was saying. We asked the nurse what had happened to him and were told he was found slumped over in his bed, unresponsive.

I had not paid attention to how much time had gone by since our arrival at the emergency room. I wondered why his wife, my sister Jackie was not there. Was she not aware something had happened to her husband? Making my way out of the room to the corridor to call her, I was asked by a doctor if I was the spouse. I replied "I was not." The doctor said they would need spousal consent for medical treatment. I told the doctor I was just about to give my sister a call. When she answered the phone, I asked if she had received a call from the care center informing her Scott was taken to the ER. She replied, she had not. I let her know she needed to make her way to the hospital. I told her the information I knew. Scott was found slumped over in bed and not breathing.

Back in the room Scott made a motion with his fingers as though he was picking up something from his hospital gown. He stretched his arm toward my friend and she opened her hand. His fingers touched the palm of her hand as though he was placing something there. He then touched her hand, folding her fingers and in a whisper said, "Keep it." MD Anderson is blessed with a fun-filled spirit about her and replied that she would certainly keep it and said thank you. We both looked directly at one another with a little apprehension and were not sure what had just happened.

Scott again started to move one of his arms, raising it up and pointing toward the ceiling. His eyes became fixated on a bright light on the ceiling. His facial expression changed taking on a rigid look. Scott's lips moved rapidly but we could not hear a sound or a whisper being spoken. It was as though he was carrying on a conversation with someone else in the room. The silent talking seemed to last only a few moments, then Scott's lips stopped moving. He was suddenly calm and more alert. I asked if he knew who we were and he smiled.

MD Anderson and I were both in agreement we had just experienced an angel in the room. Was the angel saying heavens doors were open and it was time to take him home to release him from the suffering? Or was he asking the angel for a little more time because he was not ready to leave his family?

When Jackie arrived, MD Anderson and I stepped out of the room. I was so relieved she had not seen her husband in the condition we did when we had first arrived. Family members began to show up and we decided it was our time to bow out. We had completed what God had planned for us. Scott was admitted into the hospital for a few days. It was later determined Scott's trip to the ER had been a result of his breathing tube being blocked with mucus from the lungs, preventing oxygen flow. CPR had been performed which was a care center error. He was a designated DNR patient, meaning he was not to be resuscitated.

There was silence between us as we walked through the parking lot to the car. During the drive home we quietly collected our thoughts. It was emotionally difficult to visit my brother-in-law at the hospitals and care centers. They were not fun places and we tolerated the stink from bodily fluids that hung in the air throughout the corridors and patient rooms. MD Anderson and I went there to visit because it was the right thing to do as Christians. We added joy to his day and he looked forward to our smiling faces every Sunday. We were like the entertainment team to lift his spirits and to laugh and let him know someone cared.

After the hospital stay Scott was transferred back to the care center ICU. The care given in the ICU is exceptional and more attentive with fewer patients per nurse. Scott had looked and felt his best in a long time. He was excited to show me his new shoes to accommodate the amputation of all his toes from both feet. After spending a week in ICU, Scott was returned to the normal patient care floor. Within a few days, I began to notice and hear that his breathing was deteriorating. He required more frequent breathing treatments and suctioning of the lungs.

It was Thanksgiving Day and the family did not gather for a holiday meal. In the morning, I thought I was going to the ER for my condition of supraventricular tachycardia (SVT), which is an abnormal fast heart rhythm. I had taken my medication that morning, but something triggered the onset of my rapid heartbeat. It turned out the paramedics were not called. After taking additional milligrams of prescription my heartbeat was back to normal. I had no other problem the rest of the day. All day Scott weighed on my thoughts. I decided I would visit him the next day. It would be Black Friday, the biggest shopping day of the year. Friday was not my normal day to make a visit.

When I entered his room he was having dialysis. I asked the technician what time it had started. I had visited other times during dialysis and knew Scott usually falls asleep having the procedure. It takes a toll on the body, taking several hours to complete the dialysis process. I wanted to stay a while in his room in case he woke up. I began talking to the dialysis technician. When Scott did not wake up from the sounds of our voices or from me touching his hand, I decided to write him a note. I would leave it on his bed so he knew I had been there. While writing I heard the dialysis technician talking on her cell phone. From her conversation, I learned something was not going right with his dialysis.

A familiar face entered the room who happened to be a respiratory therapist. We exchanged hellos. I have seen her many times before during respiratory treatments. The dynamics of the room suddenly changed. A doctor entered the room as well as nurses. They began preparing Scott to be moved to the ICU. The dialysis session could not be stopped at this point. Instructions were given to the technician on what procedure to follow next.

My heart sank as I stood there in the room. My eyes filled with tears. The respiratory therapist walked over to me and put her arms around me. She shared that seeing our family's love and support had given her the encouragement to do her job in this type of environment.

The ICU nurse then came over and sat down with me to talk. I could see that Scott's condition was failing and the continuation of completing the cycle of dialysis was critical. The nurse told me it was their responsibility to continue the care and to preserve the life of the patient. She said, if this was her loved one, she would make the decision to let him go. I told her I did not think my sister could make that decision. This had been her greatest fear for the last seven months of his illness. The nurse then told me she would be contacting my sister to advise her to come to the hospital.

I said Jackie was at work and cell phones were not allowed in the work area. I called my friend, Joanne who is a manager at this company. I asked if she would go to my sister's work area and let her know she needed to call me. When Jackie called, she had already listened to the message left by the ICU nurse. Her son Todd was on his way to pick her up at work and bring her to the hospital.

The hours ticked by since I had first arrived in the morning to visit. Scott never once opened his eyes or responded to my voice when I spoke to him. I sat next to his bed and held his hand, praying as I sat there alone. I did call my younger sister to let her know the change of events during my visit. Pauline was a solid rock of support and would be needed in this sorrowful time for the family. Jackie's youngest son Brian was the first to arrive at the hospital. When he walked into the ICU room, we exchanged glances. He took a seat by the wall and I let him have some time to himself.

I made my way over to him and we embraced with hugs. We had discussion if he thought his mom could make the painstaking call on her husband's life. I shared with Brian what the ICU nurse had told me. A spouse could sign the decision making over to the physician if she felt unable to do it herself.

Jackie arrived with son Todd. I stood up and helped her into the chair next to Scott. We all had always had hope. Now we could only pray for his comfort and peace. More family members arrived while the hospital staff kindly helped us. They made us feel comfortable as possible in the room with beverages and other needs we requested.

Scott's eyes remained closed, never showing a sign he knew any of us were present. The doctor walked into the room and introduced himself. Then proceeded to the opposite side of the bed from where Jackie was sitting. In a very loud voice the doctor called out, "Mr. (while using Scott's last name)." Scott opened his eyes for the first time. The doctor said,

"You are a very sick man and you are not responding to the medical treatment. Do you want us to continue helping you?" A miracle took place and Scott's lips moved. We all heard Scott say the word "no" as his eyes closed. He had just given his wife the relief and greatest gift of not having to make this decision.

The nurse spoke with the family giving us the next steps they would be doing for him. First, they would place a magnet over the area in his chest where the defibrillator was implanted. The purpose of this was to stop this mechanical device from trying to restart the heart. Next they would begin to administer morphine intravenously. They then lowered the amount of oxygen flow he was receiving. It was only a matter of time before an angel would come and bring Scott home to his Heavenly Father.

Through this all, I took away how important it is to live each day and to enjoy everyday life. All the days and hours spent with Scott over the last seven months were truly given with love and kindness. Out-of-state relatives traveled to be with the family and joined with friends in the celebration of Scott's life. My sister and her sons greatly appreciated and needed to feel their support and love. I was thankful they were there for them. I did wonder where all these people had been when Scott needed them.

I would toss pennies into a wishing well all day to have my wish granted. My wish would be to erase the memory of the tears rolling down Scott's face and hearing him say he was lonely and wished people would come and visit.

Scott

21

Not My Kid

Jason was eighteen and from a small town in Idaho with a new adventure for his life. He was relocating to Phoenix, Arizona to attend automotive school. One of the first tasks he needed to accomplish was to find a reliable and inexpensive car to purchase. The story begins with Jason calling on a car advertisement and meeting a friend of mine. Jason's available funds to spend on a car were a few hundred short of the purchase price. My friend Joanne liked this kid. She offered to let him pay off the remainder balance through labor at her newly constructed home. With a handshake agreement and title in hand, Jason drove off with the car.

Jason showed up the following weekend to begin the landscaping work. She told me he was a hard worker and was coping well with the extreme heat. Joanne was not easy to be won over, but Jason met her expectations with his positive attitude and willingness to do any task required. He worked several weekends at Joanne's house to offset the balance owed on the car.

The automotive school was not Jason's niche and he dropped out of the school program. When I was his age, I had no plan for a career path and could relate with his decision that automotive industry was not for him. I offered Jason employment with an entry level fabrication position in my company. He was a hard worker and willing to learn new skills and became part of the team. Unfortunately tardiness at work was becoming a pattern and a problem. Partying and alcohol consumption was contributing to this behavior. A decision was made to terminate his employment. This is one area of business ownership I find difficult to perform. With a small business you can easily become connected with your employees on a professional and personal level.

A little over a year passed since Jason's termination. To my surprise the shop door opened and in he came. Jason was looking for help with hardened pieces of steel needed to prevent break-ins to ATM machines for his current employer. Through discussion it was determined we had a solution for the problem.

Then an unexpected moment came when Jason thanked me for his termination. He expressed how this had helped him realize he needed to grow up. We kept in touch with e-mails, phone calls and dinner once a month to share our lives. I liked Jason, he was like my kid, even though he was not my kid.

I'm appreciative for our relationship bond, also for the trials and blessings that touched our lives together. We shared a common thread of losing our fathers without any warning. Jason attended my dad's funeral, thereby showing his respect and support. It melted my heart to know he cared so much.

The phone call no one expects to receive in the early-morning hour came with Jason's voice saying, "I'm in jail. Can you come and bail me out?" I went to the ATM to withdraw cash and then proceeded to the jail with the funds to set him free. A special part of our bond was in being there for one another.

Jason comes from a military family. He attended a town council meeting for a community project I was heading up to honor our military heroes. His presence and support meant so much to me. Jason celebrates birthdays with me when nephews some-times act as though I'm invisible. When I was his age, I did not have the mind-set to spend time with older people, even my parents. I guess getting older directs me differently about certain things in life and how to spend my time.

There were also times in which Jason and I did not see eye to eye, such as in his decision to move to California. He asked for some financial assistance before leaving and I told him no. It hurt more than he realized for me to say I was not helping him. It was not about the money because Jason did pay back his loans. I was not in agreement this would be a positive move for him. I could tell he was disappointed with my decision. California was short-lived and Jason made his way back to Arizona. A buddy offered him a job working for his company in water and fire restoration.

We all have bad habits that can sometimes drive others bonkers. Jason was chronically late and frustrating to anyone who was in a position to wait for him. Strike one, strike two and finally strike three helped break this inconsiderable habit in this person. I understand we do not have control over traffic congestion and unforeseen accidents that can delay a prompt arrival. The past three times Jason and I had met for dinner he had been late. Usually the time waiting for someone is only a few minutes, but with Jason it was in excess and no longer acceptable. Finally, I took a stand.

It was his third consecutive time of being late for dinner. From strike one, to strike two, the waiting time was increasing and my patience was wearing thin. The night of the third strike, I waited in the restaurant lobby with my eyes focused on the door each time it opened. Every five minutes that went by I told myself, "I would give him another five minutes before I would leave." While waiting I kept hoping for a text message or call from him. I wondered if he was just late again or if something had actually happened?

As the garage door was going up my cell phone began to ring. It was Jason. At first I hesitated to answer because I was so upset with him. I said hello and his voice said, "I am here at the restaurant where are you?" I said I was pulling into the garage at home. I did not give him a chance to say another word. I told him with how inconsiderate he had been while I waited a half-hour at the restaurant. Our conversation was one like we have never engaged in before. Being hungry did not help the situation.

There was a substantial cooling-down period between the two of us before we communicated again. We now have a new beginning to our story, Jason is always on time.

Mentoring Jason and loving him during these past twelve years of time has changed. "Not my kid" to "That's my kid."

> Lee,
>
> I can't tell you how much I value having you in my life, you continue to inspire me constantly. I can't thank you enough for all the kindness you have showed me over the years, it has changed the way I treat people and I'm sure countless people have been able to benefit from that.
>
> Jason

Jason

22

Heart Redemption

We have all lost someone we love and can easily fall into loneliness as our companion. The magic compass called the heart became broken when a devastating event shattered it. A horrific crash of metal and a burst of flames and you were gone in an instant. Why could I not have gone with you? When I closed my eyes all I saw was you. When the sun came up you were not there. Not another word was spoken from your lips and I never again felt your kiss.

My darkest day had arrived and all was falling in on me. I was barely holding on. Grieving and distressed, I could not imagine life without him. I did not know how or where to begin to fix the gut-wrenching pain inside of me. A defense mechanism powerfully kicked in and I began putting up walls to let no one in to break my heart. I was holding on to this thought, *How can there be hope for a broken heart?*

I lived in the past for months becoming socially withdrawn and needing to find that place to heal my grief. I decided to write Kenny a letter as a way of healing my mind, soul and emotions. I expressed gratitude for the best days shared together. In the years to come when looking back, I see your face and will always remember your contagious smile. Loss is a place to start over and I needed to move forward to live my life. I had to tell myself it was okay to let my heart and mind connect with other people. Part of a young life is going out with friends and having fun. This was the best plan for me.

Going to parties on the weekend was a typical way to gather and hang out with friends. This first party after the loss was not easy for me. The pain in my heart was still deep. I felt eyes looking at me from all directions. Many acquaintances at the party ignored me as if I was invisible. I am sure it mainly stemmed from the uncomfortable situation of not knowing what to say. Even with the awkwardness, it did feel good to be out of the house. Some of my time spent at the party was in people watching. In doing this, I took notice of a good-looking guy. I did not say hello to him. I do not think he ever looked in my direction or took notice I was there. His full attention appeared to be focused on a young lady next to him.

The following weekend friends were going to another party and I was invited to go along. Were they asking out of pity or did they really want me to join them? The eye-catching guy from the week before was at the party with some friends. This time there was not a girl attached to his side. The circle of friends I was with crossed paths with his and hello turned into flirting talk between the two of us. He was respectful and did not make any physical moves on me. By the end of the night he asked for my phone number.

He did call and we started hanging out together and going out on dates. He was fun to be with. His outgoing personality stopped people in their tracks to mingle with him. He also drove a cool car, a Datsun 240Z. This was a sporty car in my days as a teenager. This could have been what has influenced me to have such appeal for performance sports cars. Through my years, I have driven an Italian Fiat, British MG Midget and the all American "68" Camaro muscle car.

I had no doubt the suffering from a broken heart was getting better for me as the months slipped by. Undeniably our friendship was becoming a relationship. The simplicity of the physical touch of holding hands began to feel natural and comfortable once again. He was intrigued with my green eyes and the way a small single streak of brown color glazed out from the pupil. I believed his presence was making me stronger every day and the thunderstorm hanging over me was turning into a gentle rain.

I did not consider myself a party girl. The venues for entertainment were movies, parties, concerts and bars. I was under the legal drinking age for taverns. Back then driver's licenses had no photo on them. My color of hair, eyes, weight and height matched a friend. I borrowed her driver's license to gain access to the bars. The dimly lit bars required the bouncer to use a flashlight to see the driver's license information. Occasionally I had the light shined in my eyes to verify eye color matched the license. Sometimes the bouncer would ask me to give my birthdate and year for ID verification. A night of dancing our butts off to the music of a live band was fun. At the time I did not consider the use of a fake ID as breaking the law.

After one night of dancing we went to Dan's apartment to hangout. In those days we did not have cell phones. The telephone on the table began to ring. When Dan answered, I could see from the look on his face something was terribly wrong. The unthinkable happened and Dan's life would forever change. His brother had been in a fatal car accident. It was an instant flashback for me. I stood frozen in place watching Dan cry out in pain. This tragic car accident had a twist this time. I was the one looking in at another's pain and grieving. He was going to need consoling, support and love, which made me afraid and insecure. What if I could not be the super girl he needed?

New Year's Eve was staged with knowing the funeral was in a few days. The platform of a party gave Dan the surrounding of friends and much-needed hugs of comfort. We were all too young to have this kind of emotional burden cast upon us. There was expression of deep sorrow and tears were flowing all night.

Days following the funeral our hearts were covered in brokenness. Did I believe love could be the fortress to live through two tragic losses? Would we embellish each other on those days, or would we both walk with a demon? Breaking up was my only escape as my heart could not be his, not now.

Months after the breakup, Dan stopped by my house after work. We were sitting together on the front porch talking. He asked if I thought we could ever let our hearts try again. Dan confided in me, if we did not have a chance there was a girl he contemplated asking out. I touched his hand and said it was best for him to ask her out. He told me her name. Mercy me, she was a past classmate of mine from high school days. She was on the cheerleading squad and labeled in the cool kid group. He reached over and wrapped me in his arms and our skin touched for the last time.

When he pulled out of the driveway and drove away, tears filled my eyes. It was like double jeopardy and a smile came upon my face. Who would ever guess a hand-me-down boyfriend of mine was going to ask one of the most popular girls from high school out on a date? Oh yes, they did marry.

I remember receiving my first dozen red roses at my doorstep on my twenty-first birthday. We attended the same high school, but our paths had not crossed in the hallways during those years. When I was a freshman student he was a senior class member. We met at a quaint local neighborhood tavern on a summer night. He is handsome, had a great smile and glistening eyes. He stole my breath away and I was captivated by him.

Tom had a college degree in architecture. I had only a high school diploma with no career path for my future. He was a Midwest guy living at home with his parents. Their driveway was long and one day I steered crookedly when backing out of the drive. The rear tire of the car rolled on the perfectly manicured lawn. Tom's dad kept a meticulous lawn. Surely he was not going to be happy seeing his green grass flattened and pressed down in his front lawn.

One of the first things Tom helped me out with was scouting for a VW Beetle for my transportation. I was confident I would not be ripped off or purchase a lemon with his assistance. The search led to a bright orange VW Beetle in excellent condition which became one of my favorite cars.

Tom did his due diligence in asking me out and accepted the times I declined his invites. I did what I wanted to do with my girlfriends and dating was not a priority at that time. One Saturday, Tom called and invited me over to his house. He said his parents were out for the day and upon my arrival to just let myself in. He said I would find him in the basement working on some drawings at the drafting table.

Pulling into the driveway I noticed another vehicle parked next to Tom's red Volkswagen Beetle. It was a yellow Volkswagen Beetle that belonged to an ex-girlfriend. When I entered the house the music on the stereo was playing loudly. I called out Tom's name but heard no response. The root problem was my own insecurity and the fear factor of what I might see if I went downstairs unannounced. I chose to leave the house and drove back home. I had immediately thrown out a yellow flag and was making my own call for trust interference.

I was no angel, more like the wreckage of a destructive tornado in the relationship. With my fear of not being able to love or be loveable, I chose dishonesty to arm the relationship. It was a struggle for me to let the walls fall down. It was undeniable I was searching for answers and fighting my own fear to fall in love.

Tom stirred things in me like no other and I wanted to open my heart to him. I should have cried out and told Tom I was afraid because of a broken heart in the past. I guess it was not to happen for me with him. I asked myself why I could not let love shine on me? I wondered whether I would open my heart up again. I questioned why my life was marked by love but not to be in love forever.

My life changed when a friend introduced me to the love of my life. He was the one to heal my heart and His love will never leave me. I do not want anything to ever come between this love. There is only one love that never fails. *Jesus—the sweetest of love I found.*

My battles with fear were not all about my circumstances, but of the enemy dumping stuff into my head. God changed my thinking to let me take control of my life over fear. I will not let fear rule me anymore. I just do it and stand on faith. I daily put my hope in God to bring miracles for this strong female with an attitude and a little sass.

23

Father to Daughter

Once I wished upon a star for a daughter to love.

Then one day, you came into my life like a burst of sunshine.

Now every year, I watch you grow more wonderful…

and every year I love you more.

Love,
Dad

Bringing up a daughter can be a challenge and a joy—

A challenge when you think of all the things you want for her,

Like security and independence, maturity, self-confidence, and love…and a joy when she turns out like you. A daughter who possesses all of these values and more…who's so loving and loved so very much.

Love,
Dad

I'll never know the moment when the little girl I knew grew up into a woman and became a good friend, too. I only know the joy your love has brought to everything, and I hope we'll stay as close as this, whatever life may bring.

Love,
Dad

There are so many days when my thoughts are of you, when the echo of your laughter fills my mind, when the touch of your hand slips into my memory. There is a special place inside my heart where I know I can always find you. You are my precious daughter, and I love you.

Love,
Dad

A keepsake box holds these treasured words from birthday cards received as an adult. My dad did not wear his heart on his sleeve and these sentiments say how much he loved me.

Lee

24

Live and Give

My birthday is shared with Christmas in July and if you did not know the day is the 25th. Family and friends gathered for my birthday celebration at a favorite BBQ restaurant. Besides the great food, the owner of this establishment offers a ten-dollar voucher toward your meal on your birthday. There is nothing fancy about this place with its cafeteria-style dining. Patrons filled their own drink cups and selected their favorites from the condiment bar. The dining area was one big room with wooden tables and chairs for the diners to enjoy their meal.

The staff was young and worked efficiently to accommodate the line of diners formed all the way out the restaurant door. There were no alcohol beverages served at this restaurant and the barbeque food was the main draw. The homemade assortment of lemon, root beer and chocolate cake slices were decadent for desert lovers.

The busboys and girls worked fast and were continually in motion removing dirty dishes and wiping the tabletops. The restaurant was very clean, a reflection of the workers doing an excellent job. I rarely saw patrons leaving a tip on a table when departing. I suppose it may have been different if a food server had been present.

I stepped away from our table and approached a young busboy who was working to clear another table. Placing my food-soiled plate into his dish bucket, we struck up a conversation. I shared with him it was my birthday and also Christmas in July. I handed him a folded fifty-dollar bill for a tip. I received the biggest smile as he wished me a happy birthday.

Returning to my table I continued my birthday celebration with our group. From where I sat I could see him talking with two coworkers. They all had smiles on their faces. Perhaps he had decided to share his tip with all of them. One of the workers gave him a high five and they all dispersed to carry on with their jobs.

I enjoy giving with a heart of gratitude in unexpected ways and places. I seek to use what God has given me to bless and love other people. God honors obedience, be a giver. As each year passes the outer me gets older. When I look in the mirror I can embrace each new wrinkle. Joy comes in knowing, God will love me the same today as He will tomorrow.

25

Spiritual Disobedience

*L*arry and Peggy, husband and wife, soul mates and dearest Christian friends were in the midst of a remodel construction home project. Their project goal was to have their daughter and two grandchildren live with them. They wanted to give their daughter an opportunity to save money for a down payment on a house.

Friday nights rolled into a trio to share dinner together on a weekly basis with hours of talking, laughter and sometimes tears. During one of these dinners, Larry said the sharing of one refrigerator for two households of groceries was difficult to do. Three days a week Peggy worked and Larry has to fend for himself to make his lunch. The refrigerator was overpacked and it was difficult to find items at a glance, which he found frustrating. This inconvenience caused Larry to close the refrigerator door and skip lunch. This was not a good choice and should not have been an option for him as a diabetic. Peggy asked me to keep my ears open for anyone selling a used refrigerator.

I had recently received a bonus at work and believed in paying it forward to help others. I was feeling in my heart through the leading of the Holy Spirit, I should purchase a new refrigerator for them. I found one on sale with free delivery at the local handyman store. I was leaving in two days to visit an out-of-state friend and the sales price would be valid until two days after my return. I decided to take care of ordering the refrigerator when I returned back from vacation.

Upon my return there was plenty of work to tackle and accomplish after being away from the office. These tasks took high priority with my immediate focus. Tomorrow's agenda would be to order the refrigerator. The following day arrived and I did not order the refrigerator for my friends. I did not forget but instead chose to ignore the direction given from the Holy Spirit.

The following Friday, I walked into Larry and Peggy's home and saw a brand-new refrigerator for their daughter's use. Peggy shared with me how there was an immediate relief of tension for everyone when the refrigerator arrived. I was so disappointed with myself for not following the Holy Spirit's lead and not following my heart. It was not easy for me to enjoy the evening as usual because of my feelings of regret. I went home with a guilty conscience, the enemy was certainly pleased with the outcome. Before going to bed I dropped to my knees to pray. I needed to ask forgiveness for my behavior of direct spiritual disobedience.

The trio was sitting at the kitchen table together the following week. The floodgates opened wide and tears began rolling down my face. I shared my lost battle with the enemy the past week. Jesus's love gave me the courage to tell my friends the truth about not purchasing a refrigerator for them. They said they knew my heart and it was okay. I handed them a bank envelope containing money to cover their cost of a new refrigerator.

Peggy told me the money was a God blessing and was the grace of God. She had discovered a lump on her breast. With having no medical insurance and a family history of breast cancer, this money would be used to pay for a mammogram and ultrasound.

The next day I went to the market to buy my weekly vegetables and fruits. When I made the turn into the plaza, I took notice of a guy standing a few yards ahead. He was under a tree holding a cardboard sign. This guy was not standing at a main intersection where you see most folks asking for money. This location was not the best suited for high visibility or easy access for people reaching out of their car window to give him money. There was a spiritual knowing in my heart, I was going to help this person. I went into the store to shop. When I returned to my Jeep, I could see he was still standing under the tree.

I took thirty-five dollars which had been tucked inside the glove box and walked up the sidewalk toward him. I said hi with a smile, introducing myself. He replied back, saying his name was Matt. He was perhaps in his late twenties with a clean-cut appearance and his clothes were not dirty. He did not fit the typical stereotype of a homeless person. Nor did he appear in need of a shower.

He had a crutch under his right arm, supporting his leg and was wearing a black elastic support wrap around his knee. I asked why the use of a crutch, to which Matt replied, a torn ACL. I was familiar with this term from watching football and hearing of players with this same injury. I heard a Texas drawl in the tone of his masculine voice. He was tall, most likely over six feet, with a medium bulk to his build.

He was easy on the eyes, meaning a handsome young man.

I let him know his cardboard sign was too small in size. I told him I could not read the words "homeless" and "hungry" when driving by. I wanted to offer to take him to lunch but had a limited window of time. My home sits on an irrigated property and the scheduled time to open the port valve to release the water flow into my yard was within the next half hour.

There was redness in Matt's sparkling green eyes possibly caused from allergies. Perhaps even alcohol consumption from the night before. It may have seemed personal but I asked Matt to tell me about himself. I saw tears well up in his eyes and there was silence. I was moved with pity and sympathy becoming teary eyed myself. I asked if family or friends were helping. He replied in saying he was just passing through the area. I could clearly hear by his short response he was not willing or comfortable in saying much about himself.

I wondered if Matt was at the road side of life with no hope and no help. I understand all too well, how not being in a joy-filled season in life can leave you at a loss for words. He did not seem like a soul wanting to run away from me. I shared with him

I was a Christian and wanted to share the love of Christ. I handed the money to Matt and he slipped it in his pocket. I asked Matt if I could give him a hug and he agreed.

I know seeing Matt was not a coincidence. God guides and directs us to the right place at the right time. I do not give money to all standing on street corners, but use wisdom to be led by the Spirit when to help someone in my path. God had already given me peace and it was not to be my concern on how Matt was going to use the money.

I am the type of person who likes to think outside the box. Maybe Matt was Jesus in disguise and this time I had passed the spiritual obedience test. When I drove down the street I stopped the car and put down the window. Waving, I said good-bye to Matt and his good-bye came with the words, "God bless you."

I never heard God later say I should not have done this act of kindness for Matt. What's one moment of humanity worth? Everything!

26

Tree Lighting

This tree lighting at Christmas time has become a family tradition in celebrating and acknowledging our father's life and memory. In the first week of November a request is sent to the tennis director at Kiwanis Recreation Center requesting approval of the memorial tree lighting for our father. My father left his footprints on the tennis courts at this facility for thirty-one years of time.

Christmas day marked the last time my family shared with our father and grandpa before the tragic manner of death from an accident that caused subdural hemorrhage due to a blunt force head injury. Grieving is deep mental anguish and deep sorrow over a loss. To grieve is to be sorrowful, to mourn, be distressed and feel the pain. Loss is a place to start over and the tree lighting was our new beginning to Christmas.

Our family participated in a Living Tree Memorial program in lieu of flowers. This program provided us with the opportunity to honor a loved one with planting of a tree at any park or golf course in my dad's hometown. The memorial tree we selected was from the ash family. A fee is charged and this fee covers the cost of a twenty-four-gallon tree, its care, a certificate of recognition and a corresponding brass leaf. The leaf will be permanently displayed on the bronze memorial tree located in the parks and recreation office or at one of two municipal golf courses.

Our memorial tree is located within a grass-fenced area overlooking several tennis courts. This grass area has lawn chairs for those wanting to watch a tennis match. This tree provides a shade cover of protection from sun exposure for these patrons.

It is through this tree lighting, I hope my father's memory will live on for a few generations. Our family's wish is for our memorial tree to bring smiles to those who pass by and to reflect on the joy of the Christmas season.

My dad's tree is the only one in the whole park that has a Christmas light display each year. This is just another reason why our tree is so special.

Dad's Tree

27

Just Breathe

The landscape of my life is uncommon, especially when it comes to the heart.

*L*ife is not over yet, loving and being loved are what make life worth living. I guard my heart and have a heart that wants to hide. I must get back up, say good-bye to the past and where I have been. To enjoy life begins by closing my eyes and telling myself to just breathe. In the moment, I must keep a calm and undisturbed mind and heart. The complicated part of love is finding someone you like and trust.

We met in a mysterious way, was it God's plan or a silly little coincidence? What do you first notice about a person? I admire their eyes and appreciate their smile. Did I just imagine there was a connection between us? I could not deny there was a spark in my heart. Would the spark ignite into a flame over time?

My desire in a relationship is for you not only to look at the exterior of me, but to see my heart attitude. Here I am to say, I can't unlike you. I wish I knew how. No one knows what tomorrow will bring, but for certain I will always be God's girl first.

Do I listen to my mind or follow my heart? Taking risks can have great rewards. I wanted to trust and believe my heart. I'm so confused. I don't want to be scared and stay on the safe side. The normal reaction to fear is flight. A broken heart hurts and sometimes is part of the plan for what is waiting for us.

I pray for both of us to let the spirit break out and break down our walls. I know and trust God I will meet the one who deserves me.

Maybe just not the right timing for either of us. I'm sorry for both of us for missing out to know each other. What started out as friendship grew stronger for me. It took prayer and time to forgive myself for allowing my emotions to be hijacked.

28

Cheri

coincidence or a God wink? What are the odds of this ever happening at a cemetery? This wink occurred from above. Coincidences happen for a reason and this one enriched my life.

I woke up today asking myself what words do I say to a friend? A decision was made to take their daughter off of life support. The darkness of addiction was over. Life has a lot of unexpected twists and turns and Cheri's dreams had run out. Cheri was not going to grow old. Parents normally die first so this intensifies the grief. The depth of pain in an unexpected death is shocking for a parent.

It was May 22nd a beautiful spring day. Spring makes us feel happy with birds singing and seeing the amazing flowers and tree blossoms. Springtime brings everything back to life. When death occurs the person seems to just vanish.

Today was Cheri's celebration of life. A time to honor a loved one, it is also a time to say goodbye. Family and friends will all have their grief journey. Cheri's parents chose a graveside service for remembering their daughter. Grief is part of the human condition and all will face a final farewell to a loved one.

I was not sure where to park at the cemetery for the graveside service. I noticed a parking area in the far distance and proceeded in that direction to park. I locked the car and took notice of my vehicle was solely alone. The walking area would give way to locate Cheri's gravesite.

I came upon familiar faces and joined the small group attending the graveside service. A warm embrace was given to my friends and to Cheri's brother. The graveside service was led by a longtime friend of Cheri's. The Lord's prayer, Our Father who art in heaven hallowed be thy name, was the opening prayer.

It was time to express and share memories and stories of Cheri's life. It's in these words that are spoken that can bring comfort with smiles and sometimes laughter.

The woman sitting in the chair row behind mine stood and said her name was Laurie, a friend of Cheri's. Laurie shared, "we were just kids when we became friends." They met in guitar class in Junior High school. Cheri was in 7th grade and Laurie was in the 9th grade. Cheri continued with her love for music and guitar throughout her years.

At the conclusion of the service the only thing I could find comforting was hugs for my friends Bob and Donna. I wanted them to know my heart is broken for them in this tragedy that they have been faced with. I did express my deepest sympathies for their loss and sorrows. They were not ready to talk but did say thank you for coming.

I found being outside and the walk back to the parking lot seemed to soothe my soul. Something surprised me when I reached my car. There now was a car parked adjacent to where I had parked. It was a Camaro, same year and model as mine. Colors were different with mine being Inferno Orange Metallic with black stripes and the other was Aqua Blue Metallic with white stripes. These two vehicles were the only ones present in the parking lot. Standing next to the blue Camaro was Laurie the women who spoke at Cheri's service. She smiled and asked, "is that your car"?

The two of us started talking cars and I sensed a connection between us. I shared I had a 68 Camaro parked in the garage at home. This woman also was a fan of the classic muscle cars. She showed photos of her 69 Camaro, but lost ownership of the car in a break up. We talked for at least a half hour in the parking lot and it became known we were both Christians and lived only a mile apart from one another.

The discovery was also made that we both participated in car clubs. Mine was the East Valley Cruisers and Laurie's was the Camaro club. With springtime present and the dreadful hot summer months of Arizona soon to arrive, we both knew there would be no car club activity until the cooler weather arrived in October. We exchanged cell numbers and said we would hookup in the fall and attend some car shows together.

Laurie and I were amazed with this encounter of our life paths crossing at such an unexpecting time and place. Maybe it is crazy for us to ponder this as a gift from Cheri and above. Is there any other way to explain this was a coincidence? Two strangers saying hello to a new friend and one saying a farewell to a longtime friend.

In an email, I let Donna know there was a God wink to share with her from the day of Cheri's service. We planned a luncheon day and Donna said wait until then to share the God wink. It had been only a month or so since losing her daughter when we met for lunch. To help Donna with her pain grief, she decided to wear a jewelry piece of Cheri's every time going out somewhere. The story of Laurie and I brought an unexpected positive twist to also help with her grieving process.

Dealing with the death of a loved one takes time. Coping in her grief and loss, Donna joined a twelve-week Grief Share Group at a local Christian church. Donna shared at one weekly session the story of Laurie and I meeting. This God wink has helped Donna along the way. The widows and widowers had never heard of a God wink until now.

I hope you will notice your winks from God which are placed along your path for a reason. Because of Cheri, Laurie and I have become treasured friends.

Cheri

29

Antique Clocks

I always wondered why antique clocks from the 1900's spiked my interest. The only thing that comes to mind is a German cuckoo clock of my grandparents. This clock was like the forbidden fruit in the time of Adam and Eve. When visiting the grandparents home, my sisters and I were not allowed to touch the clock. Much less even look at it. Us kids were not even allowed to go in the upstairs part of the grandparents house.

We were not really liked or loved by Dad's parents. I don't remember any hugs or kisses given to us girls from them. There was one thing grandpa always did when he saw us. He would grab our cheek with his fingers and was not gentle. To be honest my childhood memory painted grandpa as a monster. We never had sleepovers at Grandma and Grandpa's.

No zoo trips or days of baking cookies with grandma. We had no heartwarming memories together with the grandparents.

Sis Jackie envisioned and fulfils the role of grandparent by providing the right blend of support, independence and so much love. Her granddaughter Leah will grow up with a positive, influential family presence because of her grandma Jackie. Sis Pauline never envisioned to see the day of becoming a grandmother due to her complicated health conditions. The blessing of the Lord is upon her and shares life with grandson Michael. My sister's quality time shared together with their grandchildren shows love.

A day at work and while taking a break, I Googled antique clocks. I replied with an email with my interest in a few clocks for sale. This clock person was a winter visitor located only a few miles from my work location. A woman from Minnesota once shared with me she was a smart bird not a snow bird. All the years hearing the winter visitors referred to as snow birds, it does make sense they are smart birds. I really liked it.

A few text messages back and forth and we picked a Saturday afternoon for viewing the clocks he had for sale. I brought along my friend Dave to the visit for security safe reasons. This clock collector was like a historian with his knowledge of antique clocks. He had many clock books in file drawers he had collected over the years. His garage was like a library of history. All this information about antique clocks would be lost and forgotten unless written within the pages of these books. He had a few tables set up with many clocks he was working on to repair and clean up.

I shared with him, I was a storyteller and a recently published author. Neither of us knew this would open up the sharing of his heartache. Why his beloved wife first? She crossed to the other side and went home to be with the Lord. He said he was told it helps folks who are grieving to write out things in a journal. So, he did.

I spent a fair amount of time with John that day. He opened up and was sharing about his fifty-five years of married life. He asked if I would take his journal writings home to read. I could not rely on my own insight or understanding of why his trust in me. He also asked if I would like to write a story of his life after losing his beloved wife.

All summer he dreaded coming back to his winter home. He had sleepless worry and concern. There was the emptiness to the point of actual hurting. How hard would it be looking at the spot where she collapsed? He did not pray asking for the need not to be required to go back. He prayed for no other help but for wisdom. He had accepted the fact it must be done. It was not only going to be heart breaking but physically very demanding on an 83-year-old.

John placed a notice in the local grocery store for clock repair. There was little tear off slips with the phone number. Can you remember those days of seeing a cork board at the grocery store with all different shapes and sizes of papers attached? Folks selling items, job postings, lost dog or cat...Then one day the internet became the link with usernames and passwords.

John receives a call from a woman who had taken a tear off slip from the grocery store. This woman had that little tear off slip for a year and a half before reaching out to him. She remembers the day seeing the bulletin board in a faraway corner of the store by the restrooms. She thought to herself, someday I may need a clock repaired and tore off one of the slips.

The lady asked if he could repair a clock for her. With only six or seven days left before leaving for sunshine, John was hesitant to take on any work. He did go over to the woman's place to look at the clock needing repair.

John was smitten the first time seeing her. He was drawn to her for some reason and he did not know how to explain it. He had been around many women since his wife's passing and there was no interest at all. If anything he was nearly repulsed by them.

This woman loved clocks and did have many of them. She showed John some of the clocks that her late husband repaired. There was also an inventory of parts and tools left behind. John was so nervous he could hardly think. He could not get out of that house fast enough. He was shaking and did take the clock needing repair home with him. It was an easy fix for the clock fixer.

Two days later he returned to her home with the repaired clock. He bravely told her the cost was a cup of coffee and a bunch of clock parts. Again, a weird feeling of attraction he could not explain. The two of them spent quite the time looking at her clocks and the tools her late husband used in repairing them.

Sarah had a large floor model of a special time clock that was not running. Of course the only way to work on it was to lay on the floor. Both were laughing while trying to get the clock running. It was a very enjoyable time and again John felt drawn to her.

A friend of Sarah's dropped off a clock for repair and he took it home. It was also an easy fix. He returned the friend's clock the following day. They had a cup of coffee and shared in good conversation. Sarah certainly wanted it to be crystal clear she was not hitting on him. He surely didn't know why she said that to him.

John was leaving for his winter months destination the very next day. Sarah asked, "are you a hugger?" He replied yes and the two of them hugged. He did not want to let her go. He said, "I hope to see you in the spring" and left.

The second day out on the road Sarah called. She wanted him to know the friend's clock was working fine and asked how he was doing. They talked for about thirty minutes. The third day out he called her. John sheepishly asked how the clocks were working. He said he was worried. Was that the real reason he wanted to call? Talking an hour with her did pass the monotony of driving down the road alone.

John told Sarah he would not call her again. He asked her to call him if she wanted to talk. He did not want her to feel pressure or that he was stalking her. Because of his past employment as a Human Resources Director, John always conducted himself in a proper professional manner. This template of behavior flowed over into his personal life with social situations.

This started the kickoff of every night phone calls between them. The calls of course were the initiative of Sarah. Sometimes their calls would last over two hours. They have talked about every subject known to man and laugh a lot! Sometimes they cry over the loss of their spouses and how lonesome it gets at times. They discovered through conversation they are very far apart on many areas of life, but also have a considerable number of things in common. Sarah is a cat lover and this stood out as a difference between them. Not a deal breaker but there was some serious concern on John's part.

John has no idea where this is going. He can say for sure; it has been unreal how the last two months of talking on the phone with Sarah has been an amazing help to him. He does not fully understand why she has shown any interest in him. With his daily disbelief and wonderment, was there a reason?

John was having a very difficult time with his thoughts about Sarah. He is full of emotions going one way and another. It had been only 9 months since Mary died. Can he even trust what he is feeling? He asked himself, what am I doing? Should I even be seeing another woman? He keeps saying, there are not enough attorneys in the county to convince me it would be okay to remarry. Marriage could mess up the estate and farm land wishes. He knew he certainly wasn't going to simply live with someone. He asks himself again, what am I doing?

They did have a rather long frank talk. Sarah is as adamant as John was, neither is going to marry again. She is very easy to talk to and he feels she has been very honest with him. They agreed to be good friends. Sarah has been such a great help to him on this miserable journey. Will time help heal both of them? Life can be full and happy at any age. Easing the loneliness is what they both found in each other's companionship.

During the visit at John's, Dave shared he has an authentic German cuckoo clock. Dave's brother Bill was serving in the Air Force and stationed in Germany. He sent the clock to the U.S.A. for Dave's family. This was a traditionally carved cuckoo clock and depicts a scene of hunting. This particular one has a beautiful detailed carved deer along with a 1-Day movement which must be wound every 24 hours. The Cuckoo clock became a noise nuisance in the home with awakening those sleeping. The clock hung on the wall in silence and collected dust for seventeen years.

Dave knew my fascination with antique clocks. He wasn't aware of my past childhood memory with the Grandparents cuckoo clock. Who could have guessed after fifty plus years my home would have a German cuckoo clock?

I gave the clock a good dusting and polishing of the wood and then placed on a wall in my home. The clock adds a look of elegance and awe-inspiring beauty to my home. Best of all is sharing life together with Dave, which brings joy and contentment into my everyday life.

German Cuckoo Clock

30

Unshakeable Trust

What happened was not the usual welcome to the neighborhood anyone expects. I had taken up residency only five days prior and had noticed many unfamiliar sounds throughout the walls of the new home.

While unpacking a box of dishes in the kitchen a new noise caught my attention. What was it? I stood frozen in the kitchen listening while I looked up at the clock to see it was 9:47pm. The noise was definitely coming from the direction of the master bedroom located at the back of the house.

Walking into the room I heard the noise again and immediately identified the sound as a window screen being removed. My mind raced knowing I may only have seconds before the glass window would be broken.

Suddenly calmness overcame me and in a loud clear voice I said, "I have a gun and know how to use it. You have three seconds." To my surprise a male voice spoke. With a quiver in his voice I heard him say, "Oh, Okay." In the silence that followed I immediately dialed 911.

The sheriff soon arrived at the front door. Together we found the side gate was left ajar. We then made our way to the back of the house. The master bedroom window screen was found leaning against the wall of the house.

The neighborhood is made up of new construction, with my house being the first on the street to be completed and moved into. With this in mind the sheriff offered helpful tips on safety. The first step was to place a lock on the side gate. The second tip is to keep the outside garage coach lights on and the front porch light. The final tip was to install a security system or get a dog.

This was a place I chose to call home and I was now frightened to stay here alone. A girl friend made an offer that I stay with her until other homes were completed on the street. I had to make a decision; would I cling to fear and leave, or stand strong not allowing myself to live in fear?

I found it difficult to believe with six kitchen ceiling lights on, the intruder was bold enough to attempt a break-in and violate my space. I later learned the builder left a few interior and the outside lights on in homes nearing completion. I suppose this person assumed no one was living at this residence.

I still could not shake the thoughts, what if I had been in the front part of the house and not heard the noise coming from the back of the home? I would have been face-to-face with a stranger in my home. I had to remind myself that most importantly, I did not get hurt but was just terribly frightened.

I questioned whether this dramatic event would trigger a past reoccurring night terror; one that awakened me from my own screams of calling out for help. How could I ever forget those words, "I'm a mother's worst nightmare." I did not know how to talk about being a victim of sexual assault. I was broken and hurting and kept it bottled up. No one knew because I never told a soul. Only God knew what I had been through. It is not simple to share this place where I had been. It was raw pain and a struggle to go through life with a deep secret. This emotional scar was secretly carried for decades and buried beneath a friendly smile. I carried shame, humiliation and embarrassment which poisoned my thoughts. I asked myself, "you say I am beautiful. Will this change how you love me?"

This was a giant to face with a stronghold in my mind. God understood my wounds and knew I should not have been treated this way. I cannot change something from my past, but I can move forward and leave the bondage behind. The spiritual weapons of the word, name and blood of Jesus are the armor to battle any giant. It was through Him, I found courage, love and forgiveness.

We all have scars, ones we inflict on ourselves and the ones others inflict on us. Abuse means miss used or used improperly. All types of abuse; whether mental, emotional, physical, sexual and verbal are damaging. But God can heal our deepest wounds. My journey to healing was to make the choice to live in God's promises instead of my brokenness. I had to lay my pain at the feet of Jesus and ask Him to heal me. Without this scar, I would not be the woman I am today.

There may be someone reading this story who has walked in my shoes and let a giant derail you. Feelings of pain, rejection, lack of self-worth and despair are something you have probably felt along the way. Whatever the wound, Christ holds the healing power. Jesus is walking toward you with His arms outstretched. He wants more than anything to take that hurting sting and crushed spirit from your life and let the ugly fall to the ground. Fear says, I can't. Faith says, but God can.

The break-in attempt jolted the writing of this story "Unshakeable Trust." I remember hearing someone say, "have trust and faith in God in the midst of your most difficult seasons." I made the decision to not park at the point of my brokenness. By taking off the mask and bringing this chapter of my life out of hiding, God wins the victory.

We all have been in broken places in life; emotionally, mentally and spiritually. We all have a past that follows us like a shadow. Everyone has a story to tell and unlike anyone else's. Each story has a different beginning, middle and will have a different ending. I want you to know that no matter how deep your pain is or what you have been through, there is hope. If you have the willingness to walk through your pain and give in to the act of intentional forgiveness, you can live boldly and stand strong.

I want to encourage you to spend time with God. His character and everything about Him will impact you in life changing ways. That fear that has been holding you back, that regret that has you stuck in a rut, that disappointment you can't seem to get over, today is the day to let it go!

Perhaps someone or something blew out the candle in your life too soon. A candle has a wick and can be re-lit at any time to show its beauty. Make the choice to enjoy the beautiful life Jesus died to give you. God's grace covers all and we are His beloved.

You may be labeled as worthless, but God's Word labels you as His masterpiece.

LOVED
TREASURED
VALUED

31

COVID-19

The nation faces an health and economic emergency of historic proportions. We come from all walks of life with different beliefs, backgrounds and political thoughts. The COVID-19 pandemic has absolutely impacted everyone worldwide. Coronavirus (COVID-19) is an infectious disease caused by a new virus. Coronavirus causes respiratory illness with symptoms such as a cough, fever and in more severe cases, difficulty in breathing. The virus spreads primarily through contact with an infected person when they cough or sneeze. It also spreads when a person touches a surface or object that has the virus on it, then touches their eyes, nose, or mouth.

I have never seen this type of an unknown situation with a invisible enemy and having a closed country in my lifetime. Our country and the world have been under a overwhelming blanket of uncertainty and trying times. This storm with a deadly virus will have every citizen being called upon to make sacrifices to fight this medical war. I will be disciplined to do my part to help win the battle with COVID-19 by following and putting into practice, President Trump's coronavirus guidelines for America to slow the spread.

Even if you are young, or otherwise healthy, you are at risk and your activities can increase the risk for others. It is critical that you do your part to slow the spread of the coronavirus by following President Trump's coronavirus guidelines for America. Always practice good hygiene and social distancing to slow down the spread of the coronavirus. Wash your hands regularly for 20 seconds with soap and water, especially after touching any frequently used item or surface. Cover your nose and mouth with a disposable tissue when you cough or sneeze. Disinfect frequently used items and surfaces as much as possible.

The coronavirus brings the sports and entertainment world to a screeching halt. Since 1911 the Indianapolis 500 has never been held outside the month of May. Race to be rescheduled in August 2020. Opening day of Major League baseball was canceled. The Japan 2020 Olympics postponed to July 2021.

The NBA and NHL season games are stopped. Music concerts are postponed and canceled. Disneyland, SeaWorld, New York Broadway shows along with Las Vegas followed suit with closing their doors.

Communities have made fundamental changes to how we live, work and interact during this national crisis. To save American lives, actions were taken to close schools, churches, libraries and do not visit hospitals, nursing homes and retirement facilities. Non-essential businesses like gyms, bars, hair salons and movie theaters are closed. Pools and parks were all closed to the public. Restaurants with a drive-up window remained open. Many companies allowed their employees to work from home to help stop the spread of the coronavirus.

Pope Francis delivers world blessing in an empty Vatican City amid COVID-19 pandemic. Faith is not dependent on physical presence. Faith is a interior strength. The Easter holiday will arrive during the coronavirus battle. Easter is the celebration of the resurrection of Jesus Christ.

This health and economy fallout have been devastating for the United States of America and for many other countries in the world. There is hope and anticipation that our country will pass from the darkness of the stress and anxiety caused from the coronavirus pandemic. I mourn for every precious life that has been lost.

Compassion and determination came together to forge a measurable difference in fighting the coronavirus. Thank you to all the heroes, warriors and angels on the front lines battling this war. Everyone of these hometown heroes deserve a round of applause and a standing ovation for their bravery.

On March 27, 2020, President Trump signed $2 trillion COVID-19 relief package into law. The largest in American history and the Bill passed in record time. I thank President Trump, Vice President Pence for the clear leadership of our country during this pandemic crisis.

With the outbreak of the coronavirus and the challenges, I learned about living well with less during this pandemic. In this time of trial and isolation with social distancing, there is so much strength when we hold onto the hope of Christ in this crisis moment.

A lot has changed in life during the coronavirus. We wear masks to the grocery store, homeschool our kids and hoard toilet paper like it's gold.

How often did we hear our mothers say, "wash your hands." Now I have heard the President of the United States of America say numerous times, "wash your hands."

PRACTICE
SOCIAL DISTANCING
STOP COVID-19

Be safe and keep the American spirit

Thank a hero of your own

My mommy is nurse Shelly.
Love you,
Leah

ABOUT THE AUTHOR

*L*ee Simonich is "True - Lee" dynamic in the arrangement of her signature sound as a storyteller and author. Her voice is strong, vulnerable and confessional with a textured tone. She takes you down a different lane and can deliver a story emotionally and with truth. Lee has a gentle willing spirit with a unique way of engaging and stirring a reader's emotions through sharing her own life experiences. She is a Christian who has opened her life to God. Lee pours her heart and soul into this book. The writing of this book was both therapeutic and a milestone marker in her life. *Looking Back* is a bold step and one of the most rewarding things she has done. Lee is a debut author with ambition and the president of a woman-owned company. Her success in the business world is the fruit of a walk of faith in Jesus.

To contact author: E-mail: leeauth01@gmail.com

CPSIA information can be obtained
at www.ICGtesting.com
Printed in the USA
LVHW070358070422
715319LV00013B/133

9 781641 140003